Balanced Literacy

Through Cooperative Learning & Active Engagement

by Sharon Skidmore
& Jill Graber

In consultation with Jackie Minor

Kagan

Kagan Publishing
981 Calle Amanecer
San Clemente, CA 92673
1 (800) 933-2667
www.KaganOnline.com

ISBN: 978-1-879097-98-8

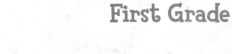

Balanced Literacy

First Grade

Introduction

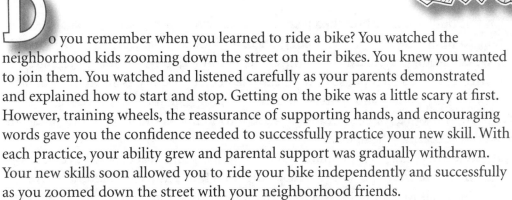

Do you remember when you learned to ride a bike? You watched the neighborhood kids zooming down the street on their bikes. You knew you wanted to join them. You watched and listened carefully as your parents demonstrated and explained how to start and stop. Getting on the bike was a little scary at first. However, training wheels, the reassurance of supporting hands, and encouraging words gave you the confidence needed to successfully practice your new skill. With each practice, your ability grew and parental support was gradually withdrawn. Your new skills soon allowed you to ride your bike independently and successfully as you zoomed down the street with your neighborhood friends.

Just as learning to ride a bike requires a series of supported steps, literacy requires guiding the learner through scaffolded instruction. The balanced literacy components provide the framework for developing deep thinkers and strategic readers. Balanced literacy increases teachers' effectiveness as they explicitly instruct through varying degrees of demonstration and practice, teacher feedback, and ongoing assessment.

[Effective teachers provide] just the right amount of support that allows the learner to assume increasing control of the task. It's a gentle dance that requires careful leading, following, and occasionally sidestepping. Gradually, as students become competent, we reduce the amount of support we offer. Intrinsic to this belief is allowing enough time, support, and feedback.

Regie Routman

First Grade
Book Organization

In this book we have provided lessons and activities to support the balanced literacy components of aloud, shared, guided, and independent practice to strengthen national standards in comprehension, word study, vocabulary, fluency, and writing. Research emphasizes that learners need to acquire skills in these areas to be proficient readers and writers. Activities appropriate for first grade students have been developed for each of the four sections in this book, incorporating Kagan Cooperative Learning Structures.

As educators ourselves, we understand the limited time teachers have to develop student materials to support the literacy outcomes for their particular grade level. One of our goals for this book was to develop teacher-friendly materials. Therefore, you will find blackline masters (cards, spinners, cubes, and mats) designed to support the activities in each section. These are located directly behind the direction page for each cooperative learning structure. You may want to consider copying these pages onto cardstock for durability. Blank templates have been included for some of the activities, giving you the flexibility to tailor activities to closely match specific literature or skills for your individual class.

The five national literacy standards of comprehension, word study, vocabulary, fluency, and writing are addressed in separate sections of this book, with the exception of vocabulary, which is included in both the Comprehension and Word Study sections.

Section 1: Comprehension

Section 2: Word Study

Section 3: Fluency

Section 4: Writing

Balanced Literacy • First Grade • Skidmore & Graber
Kagan Publishing • 1 (800) 933-2667 • www.KaganOnline.com

First Grade
A Note to the Reader

The ideas for this book are drawn from our combined experiences in the elementary classroom and as literacy coaches. As educators we are always striving to maximize learning and make every moment count as we endeavor to educate our students. It is our intention that this book will be a resource for you as you systematically think about literacy: What are the needs of my students? How can I best deliver instruction? What is the most effective use of instructional time?

When we combine balanced literacy and Kagan Cooperative Learning, our classroom practices become more purposeful and connected, resulting in increased student performance. We hope that this book will be a guide as you strive to improve instruction and enhance student learning.

A special thanks to Dr. Jacqueline Minor, our former Assistant Superintendent of Curriculum and Instruction and the present Director of Curriculum and Instruction for Kagan Professional Development, whose vision and knowledge continues to challenge us professionally. It has been with her involved guidance and encouragement that the ideas for the lessons and activities were organized for this book. Because of Jackie, this book has now become a reality.

Appreciations:

- **Illustrations:** Erin Kant
- **Graphic Designers and Layout Artists:**
  Alex Core
  Heather Malk
  Becky Herrington
- **Copyeditor:** Kim Fields
- **Publications Director:**
  Miguel Kagan

First Grade
Table of Contents

Section 1
Comprehension

Comprehension Resources

Comprehension Activities and Lessons

Section 2
Word Study

Balanced Literacy • First Grade • Skidmore & Graber
Kagan Publishing • 1 (800) 933-2667 • www.KaganOnline.com

Section 3
Fluency

Section 4
Writing

Balanced Literacy
Comprehension
Word Study
Fluency
Writing

Comprehension

Comprehension Overview

Comprehension research, as reviewed by the National Reading Panel (NICHD, 2000), suggests that students learn best when teachers are explicit in their instruction. This is most effectively accomplished when teachers tell students what they are expected to do and model their own thinking processes for the students (aloud). As students are encouraged to ask questions, discuss possible answers, and apply other comprehension strategies, active engagement increases (shared, guided, and independent).

Comprehension provides the purpose for all reading. Proficient readers are aware of their own thinking processes, making conscious decisions to apply different strategies as they read that will deepen comprehension (e.g., awareness of text organizational patterns [text types and structures], figurative language meanings, vocabulary clarification, metacognition).

Table of Comprehension Resources

Page(s)	Resources	Balanced Literacy				
		Aloud	Shared	Guided	Independent	Literature Circles
Metacognitive Awareness						
8	Metacognitive Awareness Descriptions					
10	Metacognitive Awareness Posters	●	●	●	●	●
12	Metacognitive Awareness Poster Cards	●	●	●	●	●
17	Metacognitive Awareness Poster Strips	●	●	●	●	●
22	Metacognitive Awareness Lesson Planning Form (Shared Read Aloud)	●	●			
23	Book List for Metacognitive Awareness Shared Read Alouds	●	●			

Table of Comprehension Activities and Lessons

Page(s)	Activities/Lessons	Blacklines	Balanced Literacy				
			Aloud	Shared	Guided	Independent	Literature Circles
26	**Timed Pair Share**						
26	Metacognitive Awareness Shared Read Aloud Comprehension Lesson	• Comprehension Lesson	●	●			
28	**Showdown Activity—Comprehension Showdown**						
29	Vocabulary Meanings	• Teacher Cards • Student Cards		●	●		
33	Problem-Solution	• Teacher Cards • Student Cards		●	●		
39	**Quiz-Quiz-Trade Activity—Understanding Action Words**						
40	Action Words—Verbs	• 12 pages of question/answer cards			●		
52	**RallyCoach Activity—Comprehension Retelling Mat (Fiction)**						
53	Comprehension Retelling (Fiction)	• Retelling Mat • Retelling Picture Cards	●	●		●	●
55	**RallyTable and RallyCoach Activity-Anticipation Guide**						
56	"Lady Liberty" Anticipation Guide	• Anticipation Guide Answers • Anticipation Guide Student Form	●	●	●	●	●
58	**Listen-Sketch-Draft Activity—Sketching for Comprehension**						
59	Listen-Sketch-Draft	• Example Page • Listen-Sketch-Draft Form	●	●	●	●	●
61	**Timed Pair Share Activity—Story Predictions**						
62	Prediction Mat	• Prediction Mat • Blank Story Element Cards • Story Element Example Card	●	●	●	●	●

Balanced Literacy • First Grade • Skidmore & Graber
Kagan Publishing • 1 (800) 933-2667 • www.KaganOnline.com

Table of Comprehension Activities and Lessons (continued)

Page(s)	Activities/Lessons	Blacklines	Balanced Literacy				
			Aloud	Shared	Guided	Independent	Literature Circles
65	**Jot Thoughts and Sorting Activity—Sort It Out**						
66	Prediction and Sorting Mat (Before and After Reading Knowledge)	• Jot Thoughts Prediction Mat • Sorting Mat			●	●	●
68	**Numbered Heads Together Activities— Comprehension Questions (Fiction)**						
69	"The Popcorn Dragon" Comprehension Questions	• Teacher Questions • Blank Form	●	●	●		
71	Vocabulary Definitions	• Transparency Forms • Blank Form	●	●	●		
74	Find the Book Features	• Teacher Page • Blank Form	●	●	●		
77	Creating Compound Words	• Word Sentences Cards	●	●	●		
81	**Team Line-Ups Activity—Sequencing**						
82	Jumbled Sentences Cards	• Word Cards		●	●		
84	Sequencing Events	• Event Cards		●	●		

Comprehension Resources

Metacognitive Awareness Comprehension

Resources/Materials Descriptions

How do we, as teachers, help our struggling readers improve their comprehension? We can show them how to build up their sight words, build their book list, and build time to practice reading. All of these activities are valuable but won't improve comprehension until we help students build a bridge . . . a bridge between their brains and the text.

Years of research have provided teachers with a list of comprehension strategies that good readers use while reading. Good readers are actively thinking while they read. They are aware when meaning has broken down, and they stop to fix the confusion. These strategies (Clarifying, Connecting, Deciding What Is Important, Inferring, Predicting, Prior Knowledge, Questioning, Responding Emotionally, Retelling/Summarizing, and Visualizing) become the thinking tools needed for bridge building.

Metacognitive awareness means that the reader is aware of his or her thinking during the reading of various types of texts. Through metacognitive awareness lessons, students learn to apply self-monitoring comprehension strategies. The components of balanced literacy become the avenue for the teaching and strengthening of these metacognitive comprehension strategies. Students are supported as they hear the teacher explain and use the strategies (aloud); observe the teacher use the strategies with text and participate at specific points (shared); practice the strategies with direct support and feedback (guided); and own the strategies through additional practice opportunities (independent).

Metacognitive Awareness Thinking Strategies Posters (pp. 10–11)
- This two-page poster identifies ten comprehension strategies for the teacher to use as a visual with modeling.
- It may be enlarged to use as a classroom poster or individually copied for students to keep in reading notebooks or journals for reference while reading.
- Now that students are aware that good readers think while reading, the teacher should model these strategies by stopping at various points during read aloud and explaining what she or he is thinking.
- Modeling of the use of these thinking strategies should be applied during the reading of various text types (narrative, expository, persuasive, and technical).

Metacognitive Awareness Poster Cards and Metacognitive Awareness Poster Strips (pp. 12–21)
- As the teacher reads aloud, one strategy poster card or poster strip may be held up or referred to at a time, helping to focus the students' attention on the one strategy being modeled and explained.
- These cards or strips may be made into overhead transparencies to be used during shared read alouds.
- The cards may also be attached to a Big Book page with paper clips at the point in the text where the teacher stops to verbalize her or his thinking or when the students are sharing during **Timed Pair Share**.

Metacognitive Awareness Lesson Planning Form (Shared Read Aloud) (p. 22)
As the teacher continues to model the metacognitive awareness strategies, the Metacognitive Awareness Lesson Planning Form may be used to preplan specific, targeted comprehension strategies.

Book List for Metacognitive Awareness Shared Read Alouds (p. 23)
The book list is a resource for teacher read aloud, shared read aloud, or student literature circles that focus on metacognitive awareness strategies.

Metacognitive Awareness
Thinking Strategies Posters

Instructions: Enlarge for use as a classroom poster or make individual copies for students to keep as a reference in reading notebooks or journals.

What words or ideas don't I understand?
(Clarifying)

What is important in the text?
(Identifying Important Ideas)

Why do things happen?
(Inferring)

How is it like something else?
(Making Connections)
- text to self
- text to text
- text to world

What might happen next?
(Predicting)

Metacognitive Awareness
Thinking Strategies Posters

Instructions: Enlarge for use as a classroom poster or make individual copies for students to keep as a reference in reading notebooks or journals.

What do I know about it?
(Prior Knowledge)

What do I wonder about?
(Questioning)

How does the character feel?
(Responding Emotionally)

What was the text about?
(Retelling)

What is the picture in my mind?
(Visualizing)

Metacognitive Awareness
Poster Cards

Instructions: These cards may be copied on paper or made into overhead transparencies and cut apart to be used during teacher modeling or Timed Pair Share during shared read alouds.

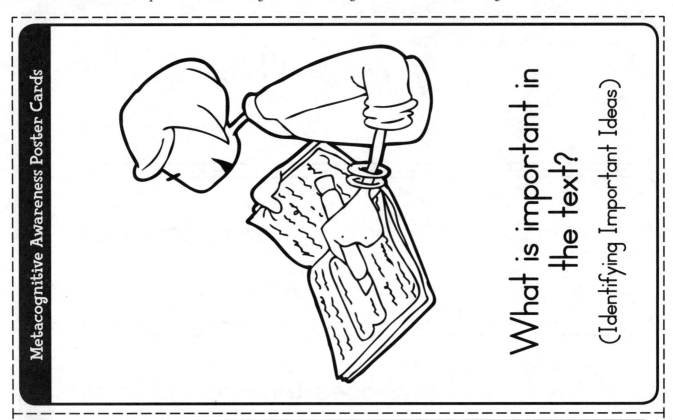

Metacognitive Awareness Poster Cards

What is important in the text?

(Identifying Important Ideas)

Metacognitive Awareness Poster Cards

What words or ideas don't I understand?

(Clarifying)

Metacognitive Awareness
Poster Cards

Instructions: These cards may be copied on paper or made into overhead transparencies and cut apart to be used during teacher modeling or Timed Pair Share during shared read alouds.

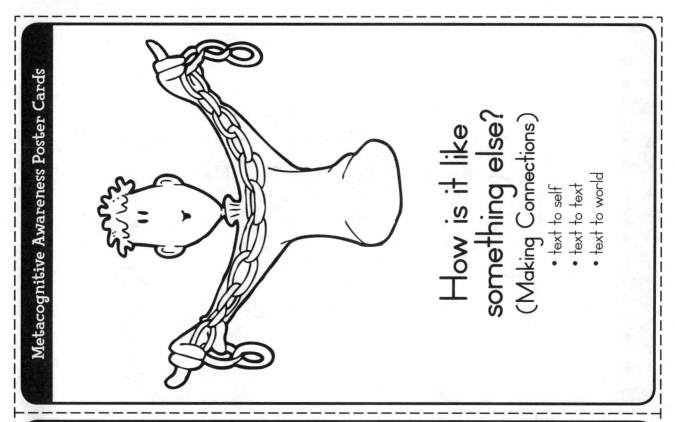

Metacognitive Awareness Poster Cards

Metacognitive Awareness Poster Cards

How is it like something else?
(Making Connections)
• text to self
• text to text
• text to world

Why do things happen?
(Inferring)

Metacognitive Awareness
Poster Cards

Instructions: These cards may be copied on paper or made into overhead transparencies and cut apart to be used during teacher modeling or Timed Pair Share during shared read alouds.

Metacognitive Awareness Poster Cards

What do I know about it?

(Prior Knowledge)

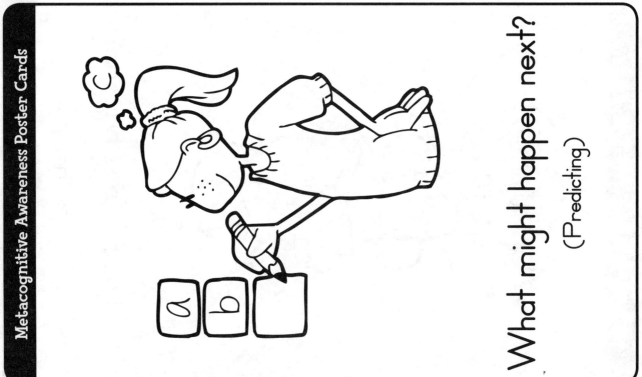

Metacognitive Awareness Poster Cards

What might happen next?

(Predicting)

Metacognitive Awareness Poster Cards

Instructions: These cards may be copied on paper or made into overhead transparencies and cut apart to be used during teacher modeling or Timed Pair Share during shared read alouds.

Metacognitive Awareness Poster Cards

How does the character feel?

(Responding Emotionally)

Metacognitive Awareness Poster Cards

What do I wonder about?

(Questioning)

Metacognitive Awareness
Poster Cards

Instructions: These cards may be copied on paper or made into overhead transparencies and cut apart to be used during teacher modeling or Timed Pair Share during shared read alouds.

Metacognitive Awareness Poster Cards

What is the picture
in my mind?

(Visualizing)

Metacognitive Awareness Poster Cards

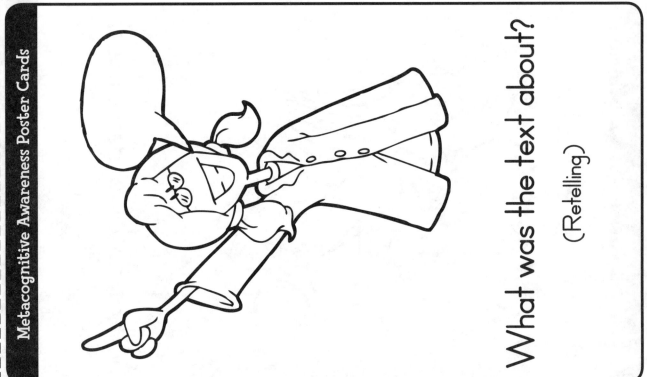

What was the text about?

(Retelling)

Balanced Literacy • First Grade • Skidmore & Graber
Kagan Publishing • 1 (800) 933-2667 • www.KaganOnline.com

Metacognitive Awareness
Poster Strips

Instructions: These strips may be copied on paper or made into overhead transparencies and cut apart to be used during teacher modeling or Timed Pair Share during shared read alouds.

Metacognitive Awareness Poster Strips

What words or ideas don't I understand?

(Clarifying)

Metacognitive Awareness Poster Strips

What is important in the text?

(Identifying Important Ideas)

Metacognitive Awareness
Poster Strips

Instructions: These strips may be copied on paper or made into overhead transparencies and cut apart to be used during teacher modeling or Timed Pair Share during shared read alouds.

Metacognitive Awareness Poster Strips

Why do things happen?
(Inferring)

Metacognitive Awareness Poster Strips

How is it like something else?
(Making Connections)

• text to self
• text to text
• text to world

Metacognitive Awareness
Poster Strips

Instructions: These strips may be copied on paper or made into overhead transparencies and cut apart to be used during teacher modeling or Timed Pair Share during shared read alouds.

Metacognitive Awareness Poster Strips

What might happen next?
(Predicting)

Metacognitive Awareness Poster Strips

What do I know about it?
(Prior Knowledge)

Metacognitive Awareness
Poster Strips

Instructions: These strips may be copied on paper or made into overhead transparencies and cut apart to be used during teacher modeling or Timed Pair Share during shared read alouds.

Metacognitive Awareness Poster Strips

What do I wonder about?
(Questioning)

Metacognitive Awareness Poster Strips

How does the character feel?
(Responding Emotionally)

Metacognitive Awareness
Poster Strips

Instructions: These strips may be copied on paper or made into overhead transparencies and cut apart to be used during teacher modeling or Timed Pair Share during shared read alouds.

Metacognitive Awareness Poster Strips

What was the text about?

(Retelling)

Metacognitive Awareness Poster Strips

What is the picture in my mind?

(Visualizing)

BOING!

Metacognitive Awareness Lesson Planning Form

Shared Read Aloud

The teacher thinks aloud as she reads to the students. Overhead transparencies of specific pages from the book are used so students have opportunities to view portions of the text. Students participate by reading from the transparencies and then discussing the use of metacognitive strategies in teams. Big Books may also be used to model and practice metacognitive awareness strategies.

Directions: Use this page to plan your lesson.

_____

by: _____

Page	Reading Materials	Metacognitive Strategies (Teacher Think Aloud)

Metacognitive Awareness Shared Read Alouds

In addition to the following list of trade books, Big Books (both informational and literacy text) are ideal for Shared Read Alouds. Some of the books on the list may also be available in a Big Book format.

Book Title	Author
Song and Dance Man	Ackerman, Karen
Sunflower Sal	Anderson, Janet S.
Little Nino's Pizzeria	Barbour, Karen
The Terrible Thing That Happened at Our House	Blaine, Marge
The Terrible Thing That Happened at Our House	Cooney, Barbara
Now One Foot, Now the Other	De Paola, Tomie
Lilly's Purple Plastic Purse	Henkes, Kevin
Chrysanthemum	Henkes, Kevin
Weberly Worried	Henkes, Kevin
Grandpa's Song	Johnson, Tony
The Boy and the Quilt	Kurtz, Shirley
The Night I Followed the Dog	Laden, Nina
No Dragon on My Quilt	Laury, Jean Ray
Bizzy Bones and the Lost Quilt	Martin, Jacqueline Briggs
Six-Dinner Sid	Moore, Inga
Babushka's Doll	Polacco, Patricia
Mrs. Toggle's Zipper	Pulver, Robin
Elizabeth and Larry	Sadler, Marilyn
Stranger in the Woods	Sams, Carl R. III and Jean Stoick
Gregory, the Terrible Eater	Sharmat, Mitchell
Walter the Wolf	Sharmat, Marjorie Weinman
Sylvester and the Magic Pebble	Steig, William
The Popcorn Dragon	Thayer, Jane
Alexander, Who's Not (Do you hear me? I mean it!) Going to Move	Viorst, Judith
The Tenth Good Thing About Barney	Viorst, Judith
The Big Boasting Battle	Wilhelm, Hans
William's Doll	Zolotow, Charlotte
The Hating Book	Zolotow, Charlotte

Comprehension Activities and Lessons

Metacognitive Awareness Shared Read Aloud

Little Yellow Chick
by Joy Cowley
Big Book- Published by Wright Group

Materials:
• *Little Yellow Chick* by Joy Cowley
• **Metacognitive Awareness Poster Cards:** Display and refer to the appropriate cards during the shared read aloud.

Metacognitive Awareness Comprehension Lessons may be used during read alouds (trade books) or shared reading (Big Books, overhead transparencies, or englarged texts). Prior to reading *Little Yellow Chick*, read a version of "Little Red Hen".

Text Page	Structure	Metacognitive Strategies Teacher Think Aloud
2	Timed Pair Share	**Questioning**: What do I wonder about? • Why do you think the Little Yellow Chick has a balloon? (*share with partner*) **Understanding Character's Feelings:** Talk to your partner about how you would feel if you asked your friends to help you with a party and they responded like the frog, bee, and beetle.
3		
4–5	Teacher Think Aloud	**Questioning**: What do I wonder about? (Read to the end of the animals' reply on page 5.) I wonder why do you think the frog, bee, and beetle don't want to help Little Yellow Chick with his party? (*Teacher Think Aloud*) **Predicting**: I think about what might happen. If Little Yellow Chick is going to have a party and he has done the shopping and cooking, I wonder what he needs to do next? (*Teacher Think Aloud*)
6		Confirm/adjust predictions. (*Teacher Think Aloud*)
7	Timed Pair Share	**Understanding Characters Feelings:** How do you think Little Yellow Chick is feeling by now? What makes you think that? How would you be feeling? (*share with partner*)
8	Teacher Think Aloud	**Predicting:** I think about what might happen. I wonder why the frog, bee, and beetle are knocking on Little Yellow Chick's door. (*Teacher Think Aloud*)
9	Timed Pair Share	**Predicting:** I think about what might happen. Predict what Little Yellow Chick might say to the frog, bee, and beetle. (*share with partner*)

Metacognitive Awareness
Shared Read Aloud (continued)
Little Yellow Chick

Text Page	Structure	Metacognitive Strategies Teacher Think Aloud
10–11	Teacher Think Aloud	**Connecting: Text to Text** Where have I seen this character before? Connect this Little Yellow Chick to Little Red Hen. I'm remembering what Little Red Hen said to her friends. (*Teacher Think Aloud*)
	Timed Pair Share	**Predicting:** I think about what might happen next. What do you think Little Yellow Chick's response will be? What makes you think that? (*share with partner*)
12		Confirm and adjust predictions.
13	Teacher Think Aloud	**Understanding Character's Feelings:** I wonder why Little Yellow Chick let the frog, bee, and beetle come to his party. I'm thinking that Little Yellow Chick planned a party and was excited about it. The text says that Little Yellow Chick was very kind. It was an act of kindness to forgive the animals and invite them to the party. (*Teacher Think Aloud*)
14–16	Timed Pair Share	**Understanding Character's Feelings:** Why do you think the frog, bee, and beetle change and ask the Little Yellow Chick to forgive them for being lazy? (*share with partner*) **Connecting: Text to Self** What can you learn from the Little Yellow Chick's kindness? (*share with partner*)

Comprehension Showdown

Teams play Showdown to master vocabulary meanings and problem-solution.

Activity Steps

1. Teacher Set is made into transparencies for teacher use on the overhead projector.

2. Each student holds Student Set in his/her hand.

3. Teacher is the Showdown Captain.

4. Showdown Captain (teacher) shows the first card on the overhead and reads it, as students follow along.

5. Working alone, students individually identify an answer from Student Set.

6. When finished, teammates signal they are ready.

7. Showdown Captain (teacher) calls, "Showdown!"

8. Teammates show their answers at the same time.

9. Showdown Captain (teacher) leads checking.

10. If correct, the team celebrates. If not, the teammates coach, then celebrate.

11. The teacher is the Showdown Captain for the next round.

STRUCTURE
Showdown

Note:
The teacher is the Showdown Captain, rather than rotating the responsibility among the team.

Blacklines

Vocabulary Meanings
Showdown (Teacher Set)

Instructions: Make one transparency for teacher use. Cut apart.

Vocabulary Meanings–Teacher Set

Mike's feet were <u>chilly</u> after playing in the snow.

Mike's feet were . . .

a) cold
b) warm

Vocabulary Meanings–Teacher Set

Kate was feeling <u>ill</u> after eating the bag of cookies.

Kate was . . .

a) well
b) sick

Vocabulary Meanings–Teacher Set

The <u>quick</u> car raced around the track.

The car was . . .

a) slow
b) fast

Vocabulary Meanings–Teacher Set

The book was <u>difficult</u> to read.

The book was . . .

a) easy
b) hard

Vocabulary Meanings–Teacher Set

The girl <u>sobbed</u> when she fell on the sidewalk.

The girl . . .

a) laughed
b) cried

Vocabulary Meanings–Teacher Set

It was so <u>dark</u> outside we needed a flashlight.

It was . . .

a) day
b) night

Vocabulary Meanings
Showdown (Teacher Set)

Instructions: Make one transparency for teacher use. Cut apart.

Vocabulary Meanings–Teacher Set

It was time for us to <u>leave</u> the party.

It was time for us to . . .

a) come
b) go

Vocabulary Meanings–Teacher Set

The towel was <u>dripping</u> <u>with</u> <u>water</u>.

The towel was . . .

a) dry
b) wet

Vocabulary Meanings–Teacher Set

We bought an <u>antique</u> toy at the show.

The toy was . . .

a) new
b) old

Vocabulary Meanings–Teacher Set

The plant was growing <u>near</u> <u>the</u> <u>ground</u>.

The plant was . . .

a) low
b) high

Vocabulary Meanings–Teacher Set

The blanket was <u>stiff</u>.

The blanket was . . .

a) hard
b) soft

Vocabulary Meanings–Teacher Set

Kim was at the very <u>end</u> <u>of</u> <u>the</u> <u>line</u>.

Kim was . . .

a) first
b) last

Vocabulary Meanings
Showdown (Teacher Set)

Instructions: Make one transparency for teacher use. Cut apart.

Vocabulary Meanings–Teacher Set

We will need to <u>drag</u> the box across the room.

We will . . . the box.

a) push
b) pull

Vocabulary Meanings–Teacher Set

Ben was <u>not at home</u>.

Ben was . . .

a) in
b) out

Vocabulary Meanings–Teacher Set

John will <u>unwrap</u> his birthday gift.

John will . . . his gift.

a) close
b) open

Vocabulary Meanings–Teacher Set

Mel's new dog is <u>huge</u>.

Mel's dog is . . .

a) large
b) small

Vocabulary Meanings–Teacher Set

They were <u>glad</u> to see their friends.

They were . . .

a) sad
b) happy

Vocabulary Meanings–Teacher Set

The moon was shining <u>above</u> the town.

The moon was . . . the town

a) under
b) over

Vocabulary Meanings
Showdown (Student Set)

Instructions: Each student needs an "a" and "b" card set. Cut apart.

Vocabulary Meanings–Student Set

a

Vocabulary Meanings–Student Set

b

Vocabulary Meanings–Student Set

a

Vocabulary Meanings–Student Set

b

Problem-Solution
Showdown (Teacher Set)

Instructions: Make one transparency for teacher use.

Problem-Solution–Teacher Set

My problem is that the chair leg broke.

A solution to my problem is . . .

a) I will give the chair to my friend to sit on.

b) I will find another chair to sit on.

Problem-Solution–Teacher Set

The problem is that someone left candy wrappers in my front lawn.

A solution to my problem is . . .

a) I will eat a candy bar.

b) I will pick up the paper and put it in the trash.

Problem-Solution–Teacher Set

The problem is that my shoes are too small and they hurt my feet.

A solution to my problem is . . .

a) I will buy new shoes that are the same size.

b) I will buy a larger pair of shoes.

Problem-Solution–Teacher Set

The problem is that the plant is wilting.

A solution to my problem is . . .

a) I will water the plant.

b) I will put the plant in the sun.

Problem-Solution
Showdown (Teacher Set)

Instructions: Make one transparency for teacher use.

Problem-Solution–Teacher Set

The problem is that I have a test at school this Wednesday.

A solution to my problem is . . .

a) I will study for the test this Thursday.

b) I will study for the test on Monday and Tuesday.

Problem-Solution–Teacher Set

My problem is that I am very tired.

A solution to my problem is . . .

a) I will go to the zoo.

b) I will take a nap.

Problem-Solution–Teacher Set

The problem is that I am hungry because I missed lunch.

A solution to my problem is . . .

a) I will eat an apple.

b) I will take a short nap.

Problem-Solution–Teacher Set

The problem is that my favorite shirt is dirty, and I want to wear it.

A solution to my problem is . . .

a) I will wash my shirt.

b) I will find new shoes to wear.

Balanced Literacy • First Grade • Skidmore & Graber
Kagan Publishing • 1 (800) 933-2667 • www.KaganOnline.com

Problem-Solution
Showdown (Teacher Set)

Instructions: Make one transparency for teacher use.

Problem-Solution–Teacher Set

The problem is that Ted drank the last glass of milk.

A solution to my problem is . . .

a) Dad will go to the store to buy bread.

b) Dad will go to the store to buy a gallon of milk.

Problem-Solution–Teacher Set

The problem was that the wind was blowing hard during the storm.

A solution to my problem is . . .

a) I tied my boat to the dock.

b) I went for a ride on the lake in my boat.

Problem-Solution–Teacher Set

The problem is that the cat knocked over her water bowl.

A solution to my problem is . . .

a) I will pet my cat.

b) I will wipe up the water on the floor and refill the bowl.

Problem-Solution–Teacher Set

The problem is that it is dark in the house because the electricity went off in the storm.

A solution to my problem is . . .

a) I will use a flashlight so I can see.

b) I will turn on the light switch.

Problem-Solution
Showdown (Teacher Set)

Instructions: Make one transparency for teacher use.

Problem-Solution–Teacher Set

The problem is weeds are growing in Kelly's garden.

A solution to Kelly's problem is . . .

a) Kelly will water the flowers.

b) Kelly will pull the weeds.

Problem-Solution–Teacher Set

The problem is that the traffic is very busy on the street.

The best solution to the problem is . . .

a) The city will put up a traffic light.

b) The city will close the street.

Problem-Solution–Teacher Set

The problem is that the grass in the lawn is getting tall.

The best solution to the problem is . . .

a) I will mow the lawn.

b) I will stop watering the grass, so it won't grow.

Problem-Solution–Teacher Set

The problem is my friend and I are hungry.

The healthiest solution to our problem is . . .

a) We will eat a box of cookies.

b) We will eat an apple.

Problem-Solution
Showdown (Teacher Set)

Instructions: Make one transparency for teacher use.

Problem-Solution-Teacher Set

The problem is the battery in my favorite clock stopped working.

The best solution to my problem is . . .

a) I will buy a new clock.

b) I will buy a new battery.

Problem-Solution-Teacher Set

The problem is my bike has a flat tire.

The best solution to the problem is . . .

a) I will take the tire to the store and have it fixed.

b) I will keep riding my bike with the flat tire.

Problem-Solution-Teacher Set

The problem is the birdfeeder is empty.

The best solution to the problem is . . .

a) I will fill the birdfeeder with birdseed.

b) I will put the birdfeeder in the garage.

Problem-Solution-Teacher Set

The problem is all the dishes are dirty.

The best solution to the problem is . . .

a) We will borrow dishes from our friend.

b) We will wash the dishes.

Problem-Solution
Showdown (Student Set)

Instructions: Each student needs an "a" and "b" card set. Cut apart.

Problem-Solution–Student Set

a

Problem-Solution–Student Set

b

Problem-Solution–Student Set

a

Problem-Solution–Student Set

b

Understanding Action Words

Teams play Quiz-Quiz-Trade for repeated practice on understanding action word meanings.

Activity Steps

1. Each student receives a card with an action word on the front and an answer on the back.

2. Students stand up, put a hand up, and pair up with another student.

3. Partner A asks Partner B to say the action word and act it out.

4. Partner B says the word and acts it out.

5. Partner A praises if the answer is correct or provides the correct answer.

6. Partner B now asks Partner A to say the action word and act it out. Partner A says the word and acts it out. Partner B praises or provides the correct answer.

7. Partners trade cards and find a new partner to quiz. The activity continues for multiple rounds, allowing students to quiz and get quizzed multiple times.

STRUCTURE
Quiz-Quiz-Trade

Question (Front)   Answer (Back)

swim

Blacklines

Action Words–Verbs
Quiz-Quiz-Trade

Instructions: Copy enough cards so each student has one card. Cut on dotted lines and fold in half.

Action Words–Verbs	Action Words–Verbs
Say the word. Act it out.	Answer
clap	**clap**

Action Words–Verbs	Action Words–Verbs
Say the word. Act it out.	Answer
find	**find**

Action Words–Verbs	Action Words–Verbs
Say the word. Act it out.	Answer
thank	**thank**

Action Words–Verbs	Action Words–Verbs
Say the word. Act it out.	Answer
dance	**dance**

Action Words–Verbs

Quiz-Quiz-Trade

Instructions: Copy enough cards so each student has one card. Cut on dotted lines and fold in half.

Action Words–Verbs	Action Words–Verbs
Say the word. Act it out. **catch**	Answer **catch**
Say the word. Act it out. **swim**	Answer **swim**
Say the word. Act it out. **speak**	Answer **speak**
Say the word. Act it out. **cut**	Answer **cut**

Action Words–Verbs
Quiz-Quiz-Trade

Instructions: Copy enough cards so each student has one card. Cut on dotted lines and fold in half.

Action Words–Verbs	Action Words–Verbs
Say the word. Act it out.	Answer
read	**read**
Action Words–Verbs	Action Words–Verbs
Say the word. Act it out.	Answer
fly	**fly**
Action Words–Verbs	Action Words–Verbs
Say the word. Act it out.	Answer
eat	**eat**
Action Words–Verbs	Action Words–Verbs
Say the word. Act it out.	Answer
mix	**mix**

Action Words–Verbs

Quiz-Quiz-Trade

Instructions: Copy enough cards so each student has one card. Cut on dotted lines and fold in half.

Action Words–Verbs	Action Words–Verbs
Say the word. Act it out. **turn**	Answer turn
Say the word. Act it out. **press**	Answer press
Say the word. Act it out. **grow**	Answer grow
Say the word. Act it out. **taste**	Answer taste

Action Words–Verbs

Quiz-Quiz-Trade

Instructions: Copy enough cards so each student has one card. Cut on dotted lines and fold in half.

Action Words–Verbs	Action Words–Verbs
Say the word. Act it out. **pick**	Answer **pick**
Say the word. Act it out. **whisper**	Answer **whisper**
Say the word. Act it out. **point**	Answer **point**
Say the word. Act it out. **laugh**	Answer **laugh**

Action Words–Verbs

Quiz-Quiz-Trade

Instructions: Copy enough cards so each student has one card. Cut on dotted lines and fold in half.

Action Words–Verbs	Action Words–Verbs
Say the word. Act it out.	Answer
carry	**carry**

Action Words–Verbs	Action Words–Verbs
Say the word. Act it out.	Answer
climb	**climb**

Action Words–Verbs	Action Words–Verbs
Say the word. Act it out.	Answer
build	**build**

Action Words–Verbs	Action Words–Verbs
Say the word. Act it out.	Answer
sleep	**sleep**

Action Words–Verbs

Quiz-Quiz-Trade

Instructions: Copy enough cards so each student has one card. Cut on dotted lines and fold in half.

Action Words–Verbs	Action Words–Verbs
Say the word. Act it out. ## write	Answer ## write
Say the word. Act it out. ## skip	Answer ## skip
Say the word. Act it out. ## shake	Answer ## shake
Say the word. Act it out. ## fold	Answer ## fold

Action Words—Verbs

Quiz-Quiz-Trade

Instructions: Copy enough cards so each student has one card. Cut on dotted lines and fold in half.

Action Words—Verbs	Action Words—Verbs
Say the word. Act it out. **spell**	Answer spell
Say the word. Act it out. **wash**	Answer wash
Say the word. Act it out. **cover**	Answer cover
Say the word. Act it out. **clean**	Answer clean

Action Words–Verbs
Quiz-Quiz-Trade

Instructions: Copy enough cards so each student has one card. Cut on dotted lines and fold in half.

Action Words–Verbs	Action Words–Verbs
Say the word. Act it out. **check**	Answer check
Say the word. Act it out. **bend**	Answer bend
Say the word. Act it out. **sing**	Answer sing
Say the word. Act it out. **yell**	Answer yell

Action Words–Verbs
Quiz-Quiz-Trade

Instructions: Copy enough cards so each student has one card. Cut on dotted lines and fold in half.

Action Words–Verbs	Action Words–Verbs
Say the word. Act it out. **hop**	Answer **hop**
Say the word. Act it out. **draw**	Answer **draw**
Say the word. Act it out. **color**	Answer **color**
Say the word. Act it out. **brush**	Answer **brush**

Action Words–Verbs
Quiz-Quiz-Trade

Instructions: Copy enough cards so each student has one card. Cut on dotted lines and fold in half.

Action Words–Verbs	Action Words–Verbs
Say the word. Act it out. **leave**	Answer **leave**
Say the word. Act it out. **count**	Answer **count**
Say the word. Act it out. **wipe**	Answer **wipe**
Say the word. Act it out. **feed**	Answer **feed**

Action Words–Verbs

Quiz-Quiz-Trade

Instructions: Copy enough cards so each student has one card. Cut on dotted lines and fold in half.

Action Words–Verbs Say the word. Act it out. **drink**	Action Words–Verbs Answer **drink**
Action Words–Verbs Say the word. Act it out. **scream**	Action Words–Verbs Answer **scream**
Action Words–Verbs Say the word. Act it out. **start**	Action Words–Verbs Answer **start**
Action Words–Verbs Say the word. Act it out. **jump**	Action Words–Verbs Answer **jump**

Activity

Retelling Mat (Fiction)

After reading the same text, partners take turns sequentially picking up a picture card, stating text information for that card, and placing it on the retelling mat.

Activity Steps

STRUCTURE
RallyCoach

1. Each pair receives a set of puzzle pieces and a puzzle mat. The puzzle pieces are mixed up and placed faceup between partners.

2. Partner A selects puzzle piece #1—"Titles," reads the prompt, and gives an answer. The student states the title. Partner B checks or praises.

3. When there is agreement, Partner A places the puzzle piece on the matching section on the puzzle mat. If no agreement is reached, the puzzle piece is set aside to be discussed later.

4. Partner B selects the next puzzle piece, #2—"Where?" (setting), and the process continues with each partner choosing the next card in sequence until the puzzle is completed.

Blacklines

Retelling Mat
RallyCoach

Instructions: Make a copy of the Retelling Mat for each pair of students.

2. Who? (Characters)	4. Beginning	6. End
1. Title	3. Where? (Setting)	5. Middle

Retelling Picture Cards
RallyCoach

Instructions: Make a copy of the Retelling Picture Cards for each pair of students. Cut apart. Partners place picture cards on the Retelling Mat as they sequentially retell a fiction book or story.

Beginning Picture Card

Beginning

Middle Picture Card

Middle

End Picture Card

End

Title Picture Card

Character Picture Card

Setting Picture Card

Anticipation Guide

Before reading a text, partners take turns marking "yes" or "no" predictions on an Anticipation Guide Form. Students read the text independently and mark their answers and page number where the answer was found on the "after reading" section. Partners then take turns sharing their answers and proving it from the text. Students are allowed to adjust answers after discussion with partner.

Activity Steps

STRUCTURE

RallyTable & RallyCoach

1. Using an Anticipation Guide Student Form, the teacher fills in statements relating to the reading, some true/yes and some false/no. (See the Anticipation Guide Answers on page 56.)

2. Pairs receive an Anticipation Guide Form and a book or article to read.

3. Before reading the text, partners take turns making true/yes or false/no predictions for each statement on the form by checking the "yes" or "no" box in the "Before Reading" column.

4. Students read the assigned article or book independently.

5. On the Anticipation Guide, students independently mark their answers and indicate the pages where the answers were found.

6. When both partners have completed the Anticipation Guide, Partner A reads the first statement and finds the related text page. Partner A states if the statement is true/yes or false/no. Partner B praises or coaches.

7. Partners alternate roles for each statement.

BlackLines

Anticipation Guide Answers
RallyTable and RallyCoach

RallyTable Before Reading		"Lady Liberty" Level 1–17 (Wright Group Publishers, Inc.)	RallyCoach After Reading		
Yes	No		Page	Yes	No
		1. The Statue of Liberty was a gift to America from Italy.	4		✓
		2. The Statue of Liberty was a birthday gift to America.	4		✓
		3. The Statue of Liberty stands for freedom.	6	✓	
		4. The date on Lady Liberty's tablet reads July 2, 1776.	4		✓
		5. Lady Liberty was brought to America by ship.	5	✓	
		6. The artist who designed the Statue of Liberty wanted it to look like his mother.	6	✓	
		7. The Statue of Liberty was built and brought to America in one piece.	10		✓
		8. Each finger of Lady Liberty is taller than a person.	8	✓	
		9. It took nine months to build Lady Liberty.	10		✓
		10. The Statue of Liberty is on an island.	3	✓	
		11. There are 142 steps inside the statue.	15	✓	
		12. You can look out of windows from the statue's crown.	14	✓	
		13. Lady Liberty holds a torch in her hand.	16	✓	
		14. You can ride an elevator in the statue.	16	✓	

Anticipation Guide Student Form
RallyTable and RallyCoach

RallyTable Before Reading		Student Name _____ Title _____ Date _____ Pages _____	RallyCoach After Reading		
Yes	No		Page	Yes	No
		1.			
		2.			
		3.			
		4.			
		5.			
		6.			
		7.			
		8.			
		9.			
		10.			

Do you have a question to ask the group?

Activity

Sketching for Comprehension

Students listen to the teacher, sketch the important details, share their sketches, then draft a main idea of the statement.

Activity Steps

1. Each student is given the Listen-Sketch-Draft form.

2. The teacher presents the first chunk of information while students listen carefully.

3. The teacher stops presenting and calls for each student to sketch the most important details in the first "sketch" box.

4. Students share their sketches using RoundRobin or Timed Pair Share.

5. Students draft a main idea statement in the first "draft" box.

6. The process is repeated for additional chunks of information.

7. When all chunks of information have been presented, students draft a summary in the bottom box.

8. Students compare their summaries with a partner or teammate.

STRUCTURE

Listen-Sketch-Draft

Blacklines

Listen-Sketch-Draft
Sample

Important to Remember (Sketch)	Main Idea (Draft)
	Max and his Grandpa feed the birds when it snows.
	The cat keeps scaring away the birds.
	They build a bird feeder.

Summary Statement:

Max and his Grandpa feed the birds when it snows. The neighbor's cat keeps scaring away the birds. Max and his Grandpa make a bird feeder so the cat cannot get the birds.

Listen-Sketch-Draft
Form

Instructions: Copy for each student.

Important to Remember (Sketch)	Main Idea (Draft)

Summary Statement:

Balanced Literacy • First Grade • Skidmore & Graber
Kagan Publishing • 1 (800) 933-2667 • www.KaganOnline.com

Story Predictions

Students manipulate cards with possible characters, settings, problems, and solutions to the text on the prediction mat. They confirm or adjust their predictions during reading and after reading the selection. Partners take timed turns listening and sharing about their Prediction Mats.

STRUCTURE
Timed Pair Share

Activity Steps

1 The teacher creates Story Element Cards corresponding to the story the class will read. (One sample set is provided.)

2 Each student receives a Prediction Mat and a set of story cards.

3 As the story is read, students are stopped periodically and given time to make story predictions by manipulating their Story Cards on their Prediction Mats. Stories can be read using:
   • Teacher read aloud
   • RallyRobin reading (partners take turns)
   • Independent reading

4 After each prediction adjustment, students are each given one minute to share their prediction with a partner.

BlackLines

Prediction Mat
Timed Pair Share

Instructions: Copy for each student.

Characters	Setting

Problem	Solution

Important Words

Blank Story Element Cards for Prediction Mat
Timed Pair Share

Instructions: Teacher writes possible story elements in these boxes and makes a copy for each student.

Story Element Cards for Prediction Mat
Timed Pair Share
Town Mouse and Country Mouse by Lorinda Bryan Cauley

Instructions: Copy for each student. Cut apart.

Town Mouse	hard work	boredom	home
Country Mouse	visit	feast	log
town house	dog	letter	girl
terror	excitement	field	

Sort It Out

Teammates cover a mat with ideas on small sticky notes before and after reading. Then they sort the ideas into categories. This is a great way to promote active listening and processing of reading content.

Jot Thoughts & Sorting

Variation

Students may work in pairs instead of teams.

Activity Steps

1. The teacher names the topic of the text selection.

2. One team member writes the topic in the middle of the Jot Thoughts Mat.

3. Students write as many prior knowledge thoughts about the topic as they can in the allotted time (one idea per sticky note). Use the same color of sticky notes.

4. Students take turns announcing one idea at a time and placing the note on the Jot Thoughts Mat in the allotted time.

5. Teams then use the Sorting Mat to organize their thoughts into categories. The categories are given titles/headings. (*Additional mat may be used by a team if more categories are needed.*)

6. Students read text.

7. Students use a second color of sticky note to record new knowledge gained from the text.

8. Students take turns announcing one idea at a time and placing the note on the Sorting Mat in the appropriate category.

9. **Team Discussion**: Students discuss the Jot Thoughts in each category on the Sorting Mat. Adjustments to information are made as needed.
   Additional Options:
   • Students may use the information on the Sorting Mat for oral retelling.
   • Students may use the information on the Sorting Mat for a written summary with each category becoming a paragraph.

Blacklines

Recall Mat

Jot Thoughts

Instructions: Copy one mat per team. Use to generate ideas for Sorting Mat.

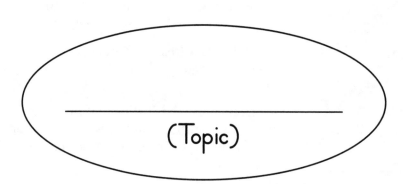

(Topic)

Sorting Mat

Jot Thoughts

Instructions: Copy one mat per team. Use to sort ideas from Recall Mat.

Activity

Comprehension Questions–Fiction

After writing their own answer to a question, teammates put their "heads together" to ensure all members can answer. The teacher then calls a number and students with that number share their answers simultaneously.

Activity Steps

1. The teacher has read aloud the same text to all the students previous to the activity.

2. Students number off in teams.

3. Teacher asks a question and gives Think Time.

4. Students privately write the answer on a markerboard or on a piece of paper.

5. Teacher says, "Heads Together!" and students lift up from their chairs to put their heads together, show their answers, and discuss until they can come up with one answer. Everyone sits down when they agree. Clear boards.

6. Teacher calls out a number. The student with that number writes the agreed upon answer on the markerboard.

7. The students with the called number hold up their boards and call out the answer simultaneously.

8. The teacher leads the class in a discussion of the answer, if needed.

9. Teammates celebrate or correct answer on markerboards.

10. Repeat for each question.

STRUCTURE

Numbered Heads Together

Variation

Students may work in pairs, instead of teams.

Blacklines

Comprehension Questions–Fiction
Numbered Heads Together
The Popcorn Dragon by Jane Thayer

Instructions: Make one copy for teacher use. Read questions as students respond on marker boards.

Comprehension Questions–Fiction

Question:
What kind of animal was Dexter?

dragon

Comprehension Questions–Fiction

Question:
Who were the other animals in the story?

elephant, giraffe, zebra

Comprehension Questions–Fiction

Question:
What was the problem?

No one would play with Dexter.

Comprehension Questions–Fiction

Question:
What did Dexter do when he got mad or excited?

His breath got hot.

Comprehension Questions–Fiction

Question:
In one word, what was the story mainly about?

friends

Comprehension Questions–Fiction

Question:
What new thing did Dexter learn to do?

blow smoke

Comprehension Questions–Fiction

Question:
Why did Dexter show off?

He wanted friends.

Comprehension Questions–Fiction

Question:
When Dexter was tired of blowing plain smoke, what did he blow?

smoke rings

Comprehension Questions–Fiction

Question:
What happened when Dexter blew rings around his tail that made him cry?

he hit himself with his tail

Comprehension Questions–Fiction

Question:
Dexter's mother figured out that he had been doing what because the animals wouldn't play with him?

showing off

Comprehension Questions–Fiction

Question:
Where did the end of the story take place (setting)?

cornfield

Comprehension Questions–Fiction

Question:
What happened while Dexter was sleeping in the cornfield?

He popped popcorn with his breath.

Comprehension Questions–Fiction

Question:
What kind thing did Dexter do for his friends at the end of the story?

popped popcorn

Comprehension Questions–Fiction

Question:
At the end of the story Dexter stopped showing off. What did the other animals want him to do?

play with them

Comprehension Questions Form
Numbered Heads Together

Book/Story/Article: _____ Author: _____

Instructions: After formulating questions for a specific text, read questions as students respond on marker boards.

Comprehension Questions Form	Comprehension Questions Form
Question:	Question:
Comprehension Questions Form	Comprehension Questions Form
Question:	Question:
Comprehension Questions Form	Comprehension Questions Form
Question:	Question:
Comprehension Questions Form	Comprehension Questions Form
Question:	Question:
Comprehension Questions Form	Comprehension Questions Form
Question:	Question:
Comprehension Questions Form	Comprehension Questions Form
Question:	Question:
Comprehension Questions Form	Comprehension Questions Form
Question:	Question:

Vocabulary Definitions
Numbered Heads Together
The Popcorn Dragon by Jane Thayer

Instructions: Make these questions into a transparency and cut them apart. Display and read each question separately as students choose *a* or *b*; *yes* or *no*.

Vocabulary Definitions

Question:
Dexter had short <u>knobby</u> legs. <u>Knobby</u> means his legs were

a) bumpy

b) smooth

Vocabulary Definitions

Question:
At the end of the story, Dexter was <u>polite</u>.
That means Dexter

a) was rude and mean

b) was kind and used his manners

Vocabulary Definitions

Question:
Could ice <u>scorch</u> you?

Yes or No

Vocabulary Definitions

Question:
If someone is feeling <u>forlorn</u>, are they feeling sad?

Yes or No

Vocabulary Definitions

Question:
Could a <u>bonfire</u> <u>scorch</u> you?

Yes or No

Vocabulary Definitions

Question:
If I am going for a <u>stroll</u>, I am going _____.

a) running

b) walking

Vocabulary Definitions
Numbered Heads Together
The Popcorn Dragon by Jane Thayer

Instructions: Make these questions into a transparency and cut them apart. Display and read each question separately as students choose *a* or *b*; *yes* or *no*.

Vocabulary Definitions

Question:

The animals watched Dexter out of the <u>corner</u> of their eyes. What did they do?

a) looked right at Dexter

b) watched Dexter in a sneaky way

Vocabulary Definitions

Question:

A chipmunk was <u>scared</u> of Dexter's smoke. Would you be <u>scared</u> of a baby kitten?

Yes or No

Vocabulary Definitions

Question:

If you are in the <u>shade</u>, is the sun shining on you?

Yes or No

Vocabulary Definitions

Question:

Would some people be <u>scared</u> of a monster?

Yes or No

Vocabulary Definitions

Question:

If you felt <u>drowsy</u>, what might you do?

a) take a nap

b) run a race

Vocabulary Definitions

Question:

If I <u>gobble</u> my food, I eat_____.

a) slowly

b) quickly

Vocabulary Definitions Form
Numbered Heads Together

Book/Story/Article: _____ Author: _____

Instructions: After formulating vocabulary questions, make them into a transparency and cut them apart. Display and read each question separately as students choose *a* or *b*; *yes* or *no*.

Vocabulary Definitions Form
Question:

Vocabulary Definitions Form
Question:

Vocabulary Definitions Form
Question:

Vocabulary Definitions Form
Question:

Vocabulary Definitions Form
Question:

Vocabulary Definitions Form
Question:

Find the Book Features

After finding their own answer to a question, teammates put their "heads together" to ensure all members can answer. The teacher then calls a number and students with that number share their answers simultaneously.

Activity Steps

1. Students number off in teams.

2. Teacher gives a direction and provides Think Time.

3. Students privately find the answer to the direction in their book and put a piece of removable highlighting tape or a sticky note on or by the answer. Teacher says, "Heads Together!" and students lift up from their chairs to put their heads together, show their answers, and discuss until they can come up with one answer. Everyone sits down when they agree. Students take the highlighting tape or sticky note off their books.

4. Teacher calls out a number. The student with that number finds the answer in the book and puts the highlighting tape on it. The students with the called number hold up their books to the page where the answer is found, point to the answer, and call out the page number simultaneously.

5. The teacher leads the class in a discussion of the answer, if needed.

6. Teammates celebrate or correct answer marked in book.

7. Repeat for each direction.

STRUCTURE

Numbered Heads Together

Variation

Students may work in pairs, instead of teams.

Blacklines

Book Features
Numbered Heads Together

Instructions: Make one for teacher use. Read directions as students find and mark book features in a book.

Book Features Direction: Find the front cover of the book.	**Book Features** Direction: Find the page where the story starts.
Book Features Direction: Find the back cover of the book.	**Book Features** Direction: Find the dedication page.
Book Features Direction: Find the title of the book.	**Book Features** Direction: Find the first capital letter on the last page.
Book Features Direction: Find the name of the author.	**Book Features** Direction: Find the name of the publisher.
Book Features Direction: Find the name of the illustrator.	**Book Features** Direction: Find the middle of the book.
Book Features Direction: Find the title page.	**Book Features** Direction: Find the first picture in the book after the title page.
Book Features Direction: Find the last word on the last page of the book.	**Book Features** Direction: Find the last picture in the book.
Book Features Direction: Find the blurb on the back cover.	**Book Features** Direction: Find the date when the book was published.

Book Features Form
Numbered Heads Together

Book/Story/Article: _____ Author: _____

Instructions: After formulating student directions, read as students find and mark book features in a book.

Book Features Form	Book Features Form
Direction:	Direction:
Book Features Form	Book Features Form
Direction:	Direction:
Book Features Form	Book Features Form
Direction:	Direction:
Book Features Form	Book Features Form
Direction:	Direction:
Book Features Form	Book Features Form
Direction:	Direction:
Book Features Form	Book Features Form
Direction:	Direction:
Book Features Form	Book Features Form
Direction:	Direction:
Book Features Form	Book Features Form
Direction:	Direction:

Activity

Creating Compound Words

After writing their own answer to a question, teammates put their "heads together" to ensure all members can answer. The teacher then calls a number and students with that number share their answers simultaneously.

STRUCTURE

Numbered Heads Together

Activity Steps

1 Students number off in teams.

2 Teacher shows the sentence with a missing compound word using a transparency and gives Think Time.

3 Students privately write the word (using the clues on the transparency) on a markerboard or on a piece of paper.

4 Teacher says, "Heads Together!" and students lift up from their chairs to put their heads together, show their words, and discuss until they can come up with one answer. Everyone sits down when they agree. Clear boards.

5 Teacher calls out a number. The student with that number writes the agreed upon word on the markerboard.

6 The students with the called number hold up their boards and call out the word simultaneously.

7 The teacher leads the class in a discussion of the answer, if needed.

8 Teammates celebrate or correct answer on markerboards.

9 Repeat for each sentence.

Variation

Students may work in pairs, instead of teams.

Blacklines

Compound Word Sentences
Numbered Heads Together

Instructions: Make transparency and cut apart. Display and read each statement separately as students write the correct compound word on their dry-erase boards.

Compound Word Sentences

The _____ flew onto a red flower.

fly	time
bed	butter

Compound Word Sentences

The _____ took off from the runway.

plane	stairs
air	up

Compound Word Sentences

A _____ fell from the winter sky.

flake	snow
rain	bow

Compound Word Sentences

A _____ landed on the rose.

lady	star
fish	bug

Compound Word Sentences

Two robins splashed in the _____ .

end	bird
week	bath

Compound Word Sentences

When the _____ rang, we opened the door.

house	bell
door	dog

Compound Word Sentences
Numbered Heads Together

Instructions: Make transparency and cut apart. Display and read each statement separately as students write the correct compound word on their dry-erase boards.

Compound Word Sentences

She got a short _____.

shine	sun
cut	hair

Compound Word Sentences

Nine o'clock is my _____.

wall	bed
time	paper

Compound Word Sentences

Let's make _____!

burn	cup
cakes	sun

Compound Word Sentences

I will _____ into the room.

tip	bed
toe	room

Compound Word Sentences

I saw the _____ wiggle.

worm	flag
pole	earth

Compound Word Sentences

We played in the _____.

paper	back
yard	sand

Compound Word Sentences
Numbered Heads Together

Instructions: Make transparency and cut apart. Display and read each statement separately as students write the correct compound word on their dry-erase boards.

Compound Word Sentences

A _____ washed up on the beach.

fish	bow
star	rain

Compound Word Sentences

The _____ splashed on me.

paper	water
fall	news

Compound Word Sentences

A _____ ate a leaf.

grass	foot
hopper	ball

Compound Word Sentences

The poodle slept in a _____.

dog	home
work	house

Compound Word Sentences

We will go to the mountains for the _____.

end	bed
time	week

Compound Word Sentences

Put the books on the tall _____.

up	stairs
shelf	book

Sequencing

Teammates each receive a card with a word or sentence on it, and they position themselves in a line so that they correctly sequence the sentence or event.

Activity Steps

1 Each team receives one set of Sequence Cards. Each student gets one card.

2 Each teammate reads his/her card using RoundRobin.

3 Student #1 states where he/she should stand in the team line-up and gets consensus from teammates (thumbs up).

4 Students #2–4 repeat Step 3.

5 Team checks the finished sequence, makes adjustments if necessary, and celebrates when correct.

STRUCTURE
Team Line-Ups

Blacklines

Jumbled Sentences Cards

Team Line-Ups

Instructions: The numbers in the corners of the cards indicate which cards belong to each sentence.

I 1	like 1	you 1	too 1
Can 2	I 2	come 2	over 2
My 3	dad 3	is 3	here 3
My 4	dog 4	is 4	fast 4
We 5	are 5	best 5	friends 5
Frogs 6	can 6	jump 6	far 6
Do 7	you 7	like 7	frogs 7

Balanced Literacy • First Grade • Skidmore & Graber
Kagan Publishing • 1 (800) 933-2667 • www.KaganOnline.com

Jumbled Sentences Cards

Team Line-Ups

Instructions: The numbers in the corners of the cards indicate which cards belong to each sentence.

Big	dogs	are	best
8	8	8	8
I	can	come	over
9	9	9	9
My	bed	is	soft
10	10	10	10
Frogs	hop	on	logs
11	11	11	11
Pigs	roll	in	mud
12	12	12	12
We	need	to	eat
13	13	13	13
The	man	went	in
14	14	14	14

Sequencing Events Cards
Team Line-Ups

Instructions: Copy one set of cards for each team. Cut apart.

The Gumball

Sequencing Event Cards–Set 1 **The Gumball** I pulled a dime out of my pocket.	Sequencing Event Cards–Set 1 **The Gumball** I put the dime in the machine.
Sequencing Event Cards–Set 1 **The Gumball** I turned the knob.	Sequencing Event Cards–Set 1 **The Gumball** Out came a gumball.

A Cool Drink

Sequencing Event Cards–Set 2 **A Cool Drink** I grabbed a clear glass.	Sequencing Event Cards–Set 2 **A Cool Drink** I filled the glass with ice cubes.
Sequencing Event Cards–Set 2 **A Cool Drink** I poured juice over the ice cubes.	Sequencing Event Cards–Set 2 **A Cool Drink** I gulped down the cool drink.

Sequencing Events Cards
Team Line-Ups

Instructions: Copy one set of cards for each team. Cut apart.

The Present

> Sequencing Event Cards–Set 3
> **The Present**
>
> My sister placed the present in front of her.

> Sequencing Event Cards–Set 3
> **The Present**
>
> She gently took off the bow.

> Sequencing Event Cards–Set 3
> **The Present**
>
> She tore off the wrapping paper.

> Sequencing Event Cards–Set 3
> **The Present**
>
> She screamed with delight!

The Haircut

> Sequencing Event Cards–Set 4
> **The Haircut**
>
> I sat down in the chair.

> Sequencing Event Cards–Set 4
> **The Haircut**
>
> The barber tied an apron around my neck.

> Sequencing Event Cards–Set 4
> **The Haircut**
>
> He picked up some scissors and began clipping.

> Sequencing Event Cards–Set 4
> **The Haircut**
>
> My hair fell to the floor.

Sequencing Events Cards
Team Line-Ups

Instructions: Copy one set of cards for each team. Cut apart.

Happy Birthday!

Sequencing Event Cards–Set 5
Happy Birthday!

My mom baked a chocolate cake.

Sequencing Event Cards–Set 5
Happy Birthday!

She frosted the cake with icing.

Sequencing Event Cards–Set 5
Happy Birthday!

Seven candles were placed on top.

Sequencing Event Cards–Set 5
Happy Birthday!

Mom lit the candles and said, "Happy Birthday!"

The Bubble Bath

Sequencing Event Cards–Set 6
The Bubble Bath

I turned on the water.

Sequencing Event Cards–Set 6
The Bubble Bath

When the water was warm, I plugged the drain.

Sequencing Event Cards–Set 6
The Bubble Bath

I placed a capful of bubble bath in the running water.

Sequencing Event Cards–Set 6
The Bubble Bath

I turned off the water when the tub was full.

Balanced Literacy

Comprehension

Word Study

Fluency

Writing

Word Study

Word Study Overview

Effective word study instruction involves both decoding words and deriving meaning from words (vocabulary). Word study allows students to take words apart while reading and put word parts together while writing. Word-solving strategies help students learn important concepts related to decoding, spelling, and understanding vocabulary. As students participate in word study activities, they become aware of relationships between sounds, letters, letter combinations, and word parts. Various cooperative activities in this book provide opportunities for students to practice application of word study skills and decoding strategies for effective reading and writing.

Following the framework of balanced literacy allows the teacher to scaffold instruction through use of explicit teaching during read/write alouds and shared reading/writing to explain strategies used to decode words and understand their meanings. Scaffolding continues during guided reading/writing as the teacher monitors and provides feedback to students applying word-solving skills and strategies. Support is withdrawn as students independently apply these skills and strategies successfully.

Table of Word Study Resources

Table of Word Study Activities and Lessons

Page(s)	Activities/Lessons	BlackLines	Balanced Literacy				
			Aloud	Shared	Guided	Independent	Literature Circles
100	Partner Word Study Activities		●	●	●	●	●
104	Team Word Study Actitivites		●	●	●	●	●
108	Class Word Study Actitivites		●	●	●	●	●
109	**Making Words Lesson Plans**						
110	**Lesson 1: "Clouds"**						
110	**RallyCoach Activity**						
110	Activity 1: Making Words	• Teacher Tranparency Form • Student Form	●	●	●	●	
112	**Find My Rule Activity**						
112	Activity 2: Sorting	• Teacher Tranparency Form • Student Form • Find My Rule Mat	●	●	●	●	
113	**RallyCoach Activity**						
113	Activity 3: Transfer		●	●	●	●	
116	**Lesson 2: "Jumping"**						
116	**RallyCoach Activity**						
116	Activity 1: Making Words	• Teacher Tranparency Form • Student Form	●	●	●	●	
117	**Find My Rule Activity**						
117	Activity 2: Sorting	• Teacher Tranparency Form • Student Form • Find My Rule Mat	●	●	●	●	
117	**RallyCoach Activity**						
117	Activity 3: Transfer		●	●	●	●	
120	**Lesson 3: "Peanuts"**						

Balanced Literacy • First Grade • Skidmore & Graber
Kagan Publishing • 1 (800) 933-2667 • www.KaganOnline.com

Table of Word Study Activities and Lessons (continued)

Page(s)	Activities/Lessons	Blacklines	Balanced Literacy				
			Aloud	Shared	Guided	Independent	Literature Circles
120	**RallyCoach Activity**						
120	Activity 1: Making Words	• Teacher Tranparency Form • Student Forms	●	●	●	●	
121	**Find My Rule Activity**						
121	Activity 2: Sorting	• Teacher Tranparency Form • Student Forms • Find My Rule Mat	●	●	●	●	
121	**RallyCoach Activity**						
121	Activity 3: Transfer		●	●	●	●	
127	**Find Someone Who Activity—Who Knows?**						
128	Rhyming words, Word Family (_at), Endings, Vowels	• Worksheet		●	●		
129	Adding Onsets, Adding -ed, -ing, Correct Spelling, Compound Words, Word Parts	• Worksheet		●	●		
130	Rhyming Words, ch/sh/th, Compound Words, Rhyming Words, Plurals	• Worksheet		●	●		
131	Find Someone Who Blank Form	• Worksheet		●	●		
132	**Quiz-Quiz-Trade Activity—Partner Word Study Practice**						
133	Word Parts	• Question & Answer Cards					
140	Rhyming Words	• Question & Answer Cards		●	●		
147	Onset and Rimes	• Question & Answer Cards		●	●		
154	**RallyCoach Activity—Coach Me**						
156	Onset and Rimes (d, l, r, s, t, w/_ay, _ip, _ell)	• Cubes • Worksheet		●	●		
159	Onset and Rimes (f, l, m, r, s, t/_ame, _ake, _ide, _ane, _ight, _ate)	• Cubes • Worksheet		●	●		
162	Onset Blends (_ew and _y/bl, cr, dr, fl, sl, st)	• Cubes • Worksheet		●	●		

Table of Word Study Activities and Lessons (continued)

Page(s)	Activities/Lessons	Blacklines	Balanced Literacy				
			Aloud	Shared	Guided	Independent	Literature Circles
154	**RallyCoach Activity—Coach Me (continued)**						
165	Onset Blends (fl, tr, gr, dr, sk, pl/_ap, _ick, _op, _unk, _ip, _ate)	• Cube • Worksheet		●	●		
168	Adding Endings (-ed, -ing)	• Cube • Worksheet		●	●		
170	Rime (_ack, _ick, and _ock)	• Spinner • Worksheet		●	●		
172	Onsets and Rimes (st, tr, pr/_ack, _ay, _op, _ick, _ash)	• Spinner • Worksheet		●	●		
175	Word Cards and Vowel Cards (Adding Medial Vowels)	• Word Cards • Vowel Cards • Worksheet		●	●		
178	Word Cards and Vowel Cards (Adding Medial Vowels and Silent e)	• Word Cards • Vowel Cards • Worksheet		●	●		
181	Onset and Rime Cards (_ack, _ill, _ay)	• Onset Cards • Rime Cards		●	●		
183	Letter Pattern and Word Cards (_ew, _igh)	• Letter Pattern Cards • Word Cards 1 & 2		●	●		
186	Consonant Digraph and Word Cards (sh, ch, th)	• Letter Cards • Word Cards 1 & 2		●	●		
189	Letter Pattern and Word Cards #1 and #2 (ar, ou)	• Letter Pattern Cards • Word Cards 1 & 2		●	●		
192	Compound Words	• Word Cards • Worksheet		●	●		
194	Onset Blends & Rimes	• Word Cards		●	●		
200	Word Endings	• Word Cards		●	●		
203	Sorting Sounds (2 sounds of *ea*)	• Mat • Word Cards		●	●		
205	Sorting Sounds (2 sounds of *ow*)	• Mat • Word Cards		●	●		
207	Sorting Sounds (2 sounds of *oo*)	• Mat • Word Cards		●	●		

92 Balanced Literacy • First Grade • Skidmore & Graber
Kagan Publishing • 1 (800) 933-2667 • www.KaganOnline.com

Table of Word Study Activities and Lessons (continued)

Page(s)	Activities/Lessons	Blacklines	Balanced Literacy				
			Aloud	Shared	Guided	Independent	Literature Circles
209	**Showdown Activity — Word Study**						
211	Word Parts	• Cards		●	●		
215	Rhyming Words	• Cards		●	●		
220	Letter Patterns–Listening Activity (ch, sh, th, wh)	• Teacher Word List • Cards		●	●		
222	Word Patterns–Listening Activity (_all, _ell, _ill)	• Teacher Word List • Cards		●	●		
224	Word Patterns—Listening Activity (_ang, _ing, _ong)	• Teacher Word List • Cards		●	●		
226	Word Patterns–Listening Activity (_ank, _ink, _unk)	• Teacher Word List • Cards		●	●		
228	**Simultaneous RallyTable or CenterPiece**						
229	Onsets and Rimes	• Word Strips • Blank Form • A–Z Student Reference Strips		●	●		
235	Onsets and Rimes Beginning Letters (s, b, m, p) (r, d, n, t)	• Word Strips • Blank Form		●	●		
238	**Numbered Heads Together Activity — Word Wall Spelling**						
239	First Grade Word List	• Word List • Word Wall Cards • Blank Cards		●	●		
247	Word Cards With/Without Silent e	• Word List • Word Cards		●	●		

Word Study Resources

Word Study Resource Descriptions

Resources/Materials Descriptions

Phonemic Awareness Resource (p. 97)
The resource lists the Phonemic Awareness terms, definitions, and examples.

Spelling Strategies (p. 98)
The goal of word study is to spell words correctly in everyday writing. Spelling strategies, which students should learn to use, are listed as a resource. Several of the Kagan activities in this book reinforce these spelling strategies.

Phonemic Awareness Resource

Phonemic Awareness is the ability to manipulate the smallest units in spoken words.

"Researchers have found that phonemic awareness and letter knowledge are the two best school-entry predictors of how well children will learn to read during the first two years of instruction." (Share, Jorm, Maclean & Matthews, 1984. Sources of individual differences in reading achievement. *Journal of Education Psychology*, 76, 1309–1324.)

The Word Study Section activities are designed to provide direct instruction and practice as students increase phonemic awareness skills.

Levels of Phonemic Awareness		
Phonemic Awareness Terms	**Definitions**	**Examples**
Phoneme Isolation	recognition of individual sounds in words	Tell me the first sound in *pup*. (/p/)
Phoneme Identity	recognition of the common sound in different words	Tell me the sound that is the same in *rat, rug, rice*. (/r/)
Phoneme Categorization	recognition of the word with the odd sound in a sequence of three or four words	Which word does not belong? *cat, cake, man* (/m/)
Phoneme Blending	ability to listen to a sequence of separately spoken sounds and combine them to form a recognizable word	What word is /t/ /r/ /u/ /k/? (/truck/)
Phoneme Segmentation	ability to break a word into its sounds by tapping or counting the sounds	How many phonemes in *bake*? (three phonemes: /b/ /ā/ /k/)
Phoneme Deletion	recognizing what remains when a specified phoneme is removed	Say *lake* without the /l/. (/ake/)
Onset-Rime Manipulation	ability to isolate, identify, segment, blend or delete onsets (The onset is the leading consonant(s) in a syllable; the rime is the vowel(s) and following consonants.)	*b-ump, dr-op, str-ing*

—adapted from NICHD, 2000

Word Study Spelling Strategies

Visualize it.

 Word

Try it several ways. Which way looks right?

Stretch it out.
Listen to the sounds.
- Letter patterns
- Endings
- Prefixes

Ask a friend.

Circle the word.
Come back later.

 Word

Check the Word Wall.

Use what you already know.
(analogy)

blue ——→ glue

Use a dictionary or spell check.

Balanced Literacy • First Grade • Skidmore & Graber
Kagan Publishing • 1 (800) 933-2667 • www.KaganOnline.com

Word Study Activities and Lessons

Partner Word Study Activities

Match My Word

Structure: Match Mine

Use stand-up folders as buddy barriers. The teacher shows Partner A a slip of paper with a word study word on it. Partner A writes the word on a small dry-erase board, which Partner B cannot see. Partner A tells Partner B how to spell the word on his or her dry-erase board. The directions may include how to form the letters, but the letter names may not be said. Partners switch roles for the next word.

Big Words/Little Words

Structure: RallyCoach

The teacher makes individual letter cards for words. These are packaged in separate bags. Partners take a bag and take turns making as many different words as they can using the letters from the bag. Each word is recorded. A mystery word can be made by using all the letters in the bag.

Computer Typing

Structure: RallyCoach

Partners use a word list to take turns giving each other words to type on a word-processing program on the computer. They change the font style and sizes, so each word looks different. Print out the words to see the finished product.

Foamy Fun

Structure: RallyCoach

Partners sit side by side. The teacher squirts a heap of shaving cream on a protected surface. One at a time, the teacher calls out the word study words. The partners use their fingertips to write the word in the foam. Partners check and praise each other.

Hand Spelling

Structure: RallyCoach

Partner A traces the letters of a word in the palm of Partner B's hand. Partner A says the name of the traced word. Partners take turns tracing the word, praising, coaching, and naming the word. Partners try identifying the word while looking and then with eyes closed.

Illustrating Words

Structure: RallyCoach

Partners take turns giving each other a word from a list. Partner A gives Partner B a word. Partner B writes the word and draws a picture to represent the word. Partner B then explains the picture and spells the word aloud without looking. Partner A praises and coaches. Partner B then gives a word to Partner A. Each word has its own box on the paper.

Partner Word Study Activities
(continued)

Inflatable Ball Spelling

Structure: RallyCoach

Use an inflatable ball with letters printed on it. (You may purchase one with letters already on it or make your own by printing letters with a permanent marker.) Partners take turns tossing the ball back and forth. When the catcher gets the ball, he or she lifts one hand and sees which letter is under it. As quickly as possible, he or she says a word beginning with that letter and spells it. Together partners decide if the word is correctly spelled and record it on paper.

Letter Ladders

Structure: RallyCoach

Partners are given a set of letter cards (one of every consonant and several of every vowel). Partners take turns making new words by changing one letter at a time. The teacher begins by giving the first word (for example, *hat*). Partner A may change the *h* to *c* to make a new word (*cat*) above the first word. Partner B may then change the *t* to *n* to make *can*. Challenge partners to see how tall they can make their ladders.

Memory

Structure: RallyCoach

Partners work together to make two identical word cards for each word on the list. Partners check each other's word cards. The cards are mixed up and placed facedown in rows. Partner A turns over two cards, saying the words. If the cards are a match, he or she removes them, spells the word without looking, and takes another turn. If they are not a match, the cards are turned facedown, and Partner B has a turn. Partners praise and coach each other.

Onsets and Rimes

Structure: RallyCoach

Partners use a container filled with individual onsets. They take turns adding these to rimes provided by the teacher to make new words, which are recorded on paper. Partners check then coach or praise.

On My Back

Structure: RallyCoach

Partner A sits on a chair without a back. Partner B stands in back with a list of words. Partner B "draws" the letters to spell a word on the back of Partner A. Partner A writes the word on paper. Partner B praises and coaches. Partners switch roles.

Partner Word Study Activities

(continued)

Roll a Word

Structure: RallyCoach

Prepare two large dice by writing onsets on one and rimes on the other. Partners take turns rolling both dice. If a word is rolled, partners praise and both write the word. If the roll does not make a word, the partner rolls the dice again until a word is rolled.

Sit and Spell

Structure: RallyCoach

The teacher writes a word list on the chalkboard. Students sit in two lines facing one another, so that only one line of students can see the word list. Students identify their partners, who are directly across from them. Partners A, who can see the words, are the "callers." Partners B are the "spellers." A caller reads a word aloud and listens carefully as the partner spells the word. If an incorrect spelling is given, the caller repeats the word and the partners spell it together. If a correct spelling is given, the partner praises. Partners switch roles for the next word.

Spelling Takes a Hit

Structure: RallyCoach

Partner A gives Partner B a word to spell by using a flyswatter to "hit" letters printed on a shower curtain hung on a wall. Partner A praises and coaches. Partners take turns giving the word and "hitting" the letters.

Study Buddies

Structure: RallyCoach

Partners take turns giving each other words to spell. A form with three columns is used. Partner A gives a word to Partner B to write in the first column. If the word is spelled correctly the first time, Partner A gives another word, which is written in a new first column. If the word is not spelled correctly, Partner B tries again in the second column. If that word is not correct, Partner A coaches by showing the word. Partner B writes it again in the third column. At any point that the word is correctly spelled, the partner is given a smiley face by the word. Partners switch roles when the words on the list have been spelled correctly or when the teacher indicates it is time to switch roles.

Water Spelling

Structure: RallyCoach

Partner A gives Partner B a word to spell on the sidewalk using a paintbrush and a container of water. Partner A praises and coaches. Partners take turns giving the word and "painting" it. (Note: Water sticks—plastic tubes with sponges on the ends—may also be used to "paint" words on the chalkboard.)

Partner Word Study Activities
(continued)

Word Search

Structure: RallyCoach

Students use graph paper to create their own word searches, including the words they are focusing on for that week. Students form partners. Using one partner's word search, partners take turns circling one hidden word at a time. Each partner has a different colored pencil. Partners coach and praise. When one word search is completed, the other one is used.

Tic-Tac-Toe—Three Words in a Row

Structure: RallyRobin

Each set of partners is given a set of word cards, a Tic-Tac-Toe worksheet, and two different colors or types of counters. Partner A picks up a card and reads it to Partner B. If Partner B correctly spells the word, he or she places a counter on any open square of the game board. If Partner B gives an incorrect response, Partner A correctly spells the word and coaches Partner B to spell the word correctly. The word card is placed at the bottom of the pile and no counter is placed on the game board. Partner A now has a turn to spell the next word. Partners try to place three counters in a row (horizontally, vertically, or diagonally). Partners celebrate.

Word Family Race

Structure: RallyTable

Partners have a letter die and a sheet of paper. Partner A rolls the die and announces the letter it lands on. Together the partners decide on a word that begins with that letter. For example, if the die lands on the letter *c*, the word *cat* could be written. Partners then take turns writing words in the word family. For example, Partner A could write *mat*. Partner B could write *flat*. Partners continue to alternate generating written words. When neither partner can think of another word belonging in the word family, the letter die is rolled again and new words are generated.

Spelling Toss

Structure: RallyToss

Partners spell a word while tossing a ball back and forth. Each partner says the next letter of the word until the word is spelled.

Word Toss Game

Structure: RallyToss

Partner A tosses a ball to Partner B at the same time as saying a word. Partner B writes the word on paper and spells it aloud to Partner A. Partner A praises or coaches. Continue by switching roles.

Team Word Study Activities

Spelling Detective

Structure: CenterPiece

Each team needs a page from a newspaper for each teammember and one for the center. Each teammember has a different colored pencil. The teacher calls out a word pattern and students look for a word on their newspaper page, which fits the pattern, and circle it. Students then trade their paper with the one in the center. Students continue circling words that fit the pattern until the teacher calls a new word pattern (examples: silent *e*, -ing ending, end chunk, "bl" blend, beginning "t", etc.).

Add On Relay

Structure: RoundTable

A team forms a line facing the chalkboard. Teammate #1 gives a word. Teammate #2 goes to the chalkboard and writes the first letter of the word, returning to the line and handing the chalk to Teammate #3, who writes the second letter of the word. Continue in this manner, until the word is spelled. If a student sees that a team member has made a spelling error, he or she may use a turn to correct the error. Teammate #2 gives the second word. (A markerboard could also be used.)

Scrambled Word Problem Solving

Structure: Jigsaw Problem Solving

Each team is given a bag with the individual letters of a word. Teammates each take a letter or letters, until all the letters are taken. Student #1 states his or her letter and where it goes in the sequence. Teammates check, coach, and move letters. Process continues with each teammate until word is spelled correctly. When the word is spelled correctly, the team receives a new bag with a new word.

Bean Bag Word Family Game

Structure: RoundTable

Each team needs a set of laminated cards with a word family written on the top (for example: ind, ant, ine), a set of word cards, a beanbag, and a different colored transparency pen for each student. Lay out the set of word cards on the floor. Teammate #1 tosses the beanbag at the cards. He or she picks up the card that the beanbag landed on, says the word, and uses a transparency pen to write the word on the correct word family card. The word card goes in a discard pile. The other teammates take turns tossing the beanbag and writing the words on the word family cards.

Word Family Lists

Structure: Jot Thoughts

Each student writes one word per slip of paper and announces the word before placing it on the table. Each added word needs to be new. Teammates cover the table with words belonging to a word family written on slips of paper (omit commas in this sentence).

Team Word Study Activities
(continued)

Colorful Team Spelling

Structure: RoundTable

Each team member has a different colored pencil or marker. The teacher gives a word. The team passes a paper around the table. Each student adds one letter to spell the word and passes the paper on to the next student until the word is spelled.

Do You Know My Word?

Structure: Showdown

One teammate spells aloud a word. Once the word is spelled, teammates pick up a marker and spell the word on individual dry-erase boards. When the Showdown Captain calls, "Showdown," teammates hold up their boards and show their spellings and name the word. They then celebrate or coach.

Sentence Writing

Structure: RoundTable

Each student on the team has a different colored pencil. Each person adds a word to a paper, which is passed around the table. The words need to form a complete sentence. When the sentence is completed, the sentence is read to the other teams. Each word study word for the week that is used correctly in the sentence is worth one point for the class goal.

Find the Errors

Structure: Simultaneous RoundTable

Each team has four teacher-made sentence strips with spelling errors (one for each student). Each student has a different colored pencil. The papers are passed around the table, with each student correcting one error before passing the paper to the next student. Keep passing the sentences around until all the errors have been corrected.

Guess the Letters

Structure: Talking Chips

Use a large dry-erase board or chalkboard that all team members can see. Teammate #1 looks at a list of words and chooses one word. He or she makes a line for each letter of the word (_ _ _ _). The other team members take turns putting a Talking Chip in the middle of the table and guessing a letter or the word. If the word is not guessed and all the Talking Chips have been used, teammates pick up their Talking Chips and begin guessing again. When the word has been identified, Teammate #2 chooses a new word. Continue until all teammates have had an opportunity to choose a word.

Word Family Web

Structure: RoundTable

Each team works together to create a word family web. A large piece of paper is placed in the center of the team with a word family written in the middle (for example: ick, ate, ip). Each student has a different colored marker. Teammates take turns adding a word to the word family web. The team needs to agree on the spelling of the word before the next person writes.

Team Word Study Activities

(continued)

Body Spelling

Structure: Team Formations

Each team receives a word on a card. Their task is to use their bodies to spell the word. Each person on the team must be part of the spelling. Other teams guess what word was spelled.

Movement Spelling

Structure: Team Formations

The teacher calls out a word. Each team decides on a repetitive movement to use with each letter. For example, one team may decide to hop on one foot for each letter of the word as they spell it. Teams spell the word for the other teams, after practicing their words and movements at least three times. (Variation: Teams may use a different movement for each letter of the word.)

Spelling Cheerleaders

Structure: Team Formations

Students in teams act out the given word with their bodies, showing the tall letters (stretching tall with hands over heads), short letters (putting arms straight out or on hips), and tail letters (squatting or touching toes). For example, "Give me a ____. Give me an ____. Give me a __."

Machine Spelling

Structure: Team Line-Ups

Each student on a team becomes one letter of the word being spelled. They line up in order. The word is spelled orally with each student saying his or her letter while making a body motion. The team becomes a "word machine." Teams demonstrate their machines to the other teams.

Word Line-Ups

Structure: Team Line-Ups

Each team receives a stack of scrambled letters, which spell a word. Each teammate takes one of the letters. (Teammates may need to take more than one letter or share a letter, depending on the length of the word.) Each team tries to be the first to line up, holding the letters in the correct order to spell the word. (If a team member has two letters, which are not positioned side by side in the word, the team will need to be creative in solving the problem.) Teams share their words with other teams.

Word Practice

Structure: Team-Pair-Solo

Teams work together to spell a word. Then teams divide into pairs and spell the same word. They compare with the other pair. Finally, individuals spell the word. They come back together as a team and compare. They celebrate or coach and begin the process with a new word.

Team Word Study Activities

(continued)

Spelling Word Collage

Structure: Team Word-Webbing

Roll out a large piece of paper on the floor or tape one to a wall for each team. Each student has a different colored marker. In a set amount of time, each student tries to fit in as many word study words as possible on the paper to create a colorful word collage.

Pick a Letter, Any Letter

Structure: Think-Write-RoundRobin

Each team has a bag of letters. Teammate #1 chooses a letter from the bag without looking and announces the letter to the team, placing it in the middle. Each student thinks about possible words beginning with that letter and then makes a list of words beginning with that letter on individual dry-erase boards. Time is called after a preset time limit. Teammates take turns RoundRobin sharing one of the words on their lists. If a shared word is also on their lists, students may put a mark by it. Words shared aloud must be new words not previously shared. Continue sharing until all new words have been shared. If a teammate does not have a new word on the list to share, he or she may try to come up with another word.

Spelling Walk

Structure: Traveling Heads Together

Teams huddle to make sure all can spell a given word correctly. Use dry-erase boards to practice writing the word. When everyone is confident they can spell the word, the dry-erase boards are cleared and the team sits down. The teacher calls a number; the student with that number travels to a new team with his or her cleared dry-erase board and a marker. At the new team, the student shares the spelling of the word by writing it on the dry-erase board.

Spelling Toss

Structure: Turn Toss

Teammates toss a ball to each other. As each teammate catches the ball, he or she contributes a letter to the spelling of a word called out by the teacher. Teammates continue until the word is spelled. The teacher then gives a new word.

Class Word Study Activities

Add a Word to My Family

Structure: Find Someone Who

Students have bingo sheets. At the top they put a word given by the teacher. They circulate throughout the room looking for someone who can add a word to a square on their paper and sign his or her name below the added word. The word needs to belong to the same family as the given word and needs to be one that is not already on the paper.

Spell My Word

Structure: Inside-Outside Circle

Students form two circles facing each other. Each student has a word list. As either the outside or the inside circle moves one space, students face new partners. Partners take turns having their partner spell a word from the list. Rotate.

What's My Word?

Structure: Who Am I?

Students attempt to determine their secret word (taped on their back) by circulating and asking "yes/no" questions of classmates. They are allowed three questions per classmate (or unlimited questions until they receive a "no" response). They then find a new classmate to question. When the student guesses his or her word, the student becomes a consultant to give clues to those who have not yet found their identity.

Jumping Words

Structure: Take Off, Touch Down

Give each student a word card. The teacher calls out a vowel sound. If the student's word contains the vowel sound, he or she stands or jumps up. Standing students share their words simultaneously. Teacher and class check for accuracy. The teacher continues to call vowel sounds as students listen for the vowel sound in their words. Variation: The teacher calls out a word and students jump up when they hear a word that rhymes with the word on their word card.

How Many?

Structure: Mix-Freeze-Group

Students make groups with a specific number of students corresponding to answers to questions, asked by the teacher, such as:
  • # of total letters in a given word
  • # of vowels in a word
  • # of a specific letter in a word
  • # of syllables in a word
(For example, if the answer to the question is four, when the teacher calls, "Show me," students show the number 4 with their fingers on their chests, quickly form groups of four, and kneel down. Students not finding a group should meet in a predetermined part of the room in "Lost and Found.")

Balanced Literacy • First Grade • Skidmore & Graber
Kagan Publishing • 1 (800) 933-2667 • www.KaganOnline.com

Making Words Lesson Plans

On the following pages are three lessons designed to help students think about the sounds they hear in words and the letter patterns that make up those sounds. They all involve making words from one longer word. The steps for the three lessons are the same. In each of the three lessons, students proceed through three activities:

- **Activity 1: Making Words** (RallyCoach)
- **Activity 2: Sorting** (Find My Rule)
- **Activity 3: Transfer** (RallyCoach)

Since the steps are the same for all three lessons, we will provide a full description of Lesson 1, then just provide the necessary substitutions for Lessons 2 and 3.

Each lesson has its own set of blacklines, but they all share the Find My Rule Mat on page 124. Also, you will find two forms to plan and create your own Making Words lessons.

- **Making Words Planning Form** (p. 125)
- **Making Words Student Form** (p. 126)

The Magic Word
When done with each lesson, challenge pairs to see if they can discover the "Magic Word." The magic word is the word made from all the letters from each set of student letters.
The magic words from each lesson is:
Lesson 1: clouds
Lesson 2: jumping
Lesson 3: peanuts

Helpful Hints:
- These activities may be done in one day or two days at the beginning of the week. Making Words may be done on day one, and the Sorting and Transfer activities on day two.
- Mailing envelopes or plastic sandwich baggies will help students keep their materials organized and accessible.
- These activities are most beneficial when the teacher selects or designs lessons that reinforce letter patterns the students need to know or strengthen for their reading and writing.
- All letters on the Making Words form are put in alphabetical order with vowels first, followed by consonants.

Making Words Lessons

Lessons

Making Words
Lesson 1: "Clouds"

Activity 1: Making Words

In pairs, students take turns manipulating letter cards to make words.

Activity 1 Steps

1. The teacher makes a transparency of the Making Words (Clouds) page and cuts out the letters and words.

2. Each pair receives one set of the following letters: *o, u, c, d, l, s* (the letters form the word *clouds*) from the blackline.

3. The teacher asks students to make words as described in the table on page 111, Words to Make from *Clouds*. The teacher reviews the teaching points as indicated on the table.

4. Partner A makes the first word, while Partner B coaches if necessary.

5. The teacher makes the word on the overhead projector.

6. Students write the word in a box on their student form. They will use these words in Activity 2.

7. Partners take turns for each new word and the process is repeated.

STRUCTURE
RallyCoach

Blacklines

Words to Make from *Clouds*

Directions	Word	Teaching Point
Make: *so*	so	
Make: *do*	do	Discuss the two sounds of /o/.
Make: *sod* *The sod house was made of dirt and grass.*	sod	Discuss the short /o/.
Make: *old*	old	'Old' is a word but it can also be a letter pattern.
Add an 's' to the beginning.	sold	Discuss using /old/ to decode or write.
Make: *cold*	cold	Decoding by covering up from the vowel to the end of the word, saying the beginning sound, uncovering letter pattern, and saying it. Put it all together.
Use the same letters and make: *clod*	clod	
Make it plural: more than one *clod*	clods	Discuss plural endings.
Use the same letters and make *scold*.	scold	What letter pattern helped you? Discuss decoding: cover up from the vowel to the end, say blend, uncover, and blend it together.
Make: *loud*	loud	Discuss /ou/ letter pattern.
Use all the letters to make the magic word.	clouds	Discuss using /ou/ letter pattern and blends to write/read.

Activity 2: Sorting

The teacher places words in two different columns on the overhead projector. The challenge is for students to discover the teacher's rules for sorting the words this way. This activity draws the students' attention to visual clues and letter patterns.

Activity 2 Steps

STRUCTURE
Find My Rule

Ideas for Rules

- **/old/ word pattern**
- **/ou/ letter pattern**
- **words that begin with blends**
- **long /o/ sound**
- **short /o/ sound**

1. The teacher makes a transparency of the Find My Rule Mat (page 124).

2. The teacher decides on a "rule" to place words in the two different columns of the Mat. For the example below, the rule is **/old/ word pattern.**

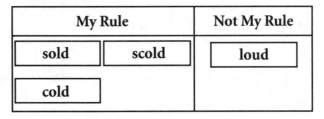

My Rule		Not My Rule
sold	scold	loud
cold		

3. The teacher places one word in each column, and asks, "What is my rule?"

4. Students RallyRobin with their shoulder partners to determine what the rule may be.

5. The teacher adds the next two words, one in each column, and asks again, "What is my rule?"

6. Students RallyRobin again.

7. This continues until students think they know the rule. The teacher calls on students to verbalize the rule. If correct, the teacher congratulates the students, if incorrect the process continues.

8. When done, the activity may be repeated with a new rule. Other rule examples are listed at left.

9. After practice, students can cut apart their word boxes from Activity 1, step 6. They can create their own word sorts and have a partner find the rule.

Activity 3: Transfer

The teacher displays a word card on the overhead projector and discusses the letter pattern. Then the teacher says, "If you can spell this word, you can also spell...." Students work in pairs to spell the new word. This activity helps students "use what they know" from one word and transfer it to a new word that they are trying to read or write.

STRUCTURE
RallyCoach

Activity 3 Steps

1. The teacher places a word card on the overhead projector.

2. The teacher states, "If you can spell this word, you can also spell...." (See the examples below.)

3. Partner A spells the word while Partner B watches, checks, and coaches as needed.

4. The teacher spells the new word for the class, and students praise their partners for correct spelling.

5. Students switch roles of Speller and Coach for each new word.

Using What You Know	
If you can spell...	Then you can spell...
sod	nod, rod, plod
cold	bold, gold, hold, told
cloud	proud, loud

Making Words (*Clouds*)
Teacher Transparency Form

Instructions: Make a transparency of this page. Cut out letters and words to use during Activity 1: Making Words and with Activity 2: Sorting.

	old	clods					
s	sod	clod	clouds				
l							
l							
d	do	cold	loud				
c							
u	so	sold	scold				
o							

Balanced Literacy • First Grade • Skidmore & Graber
Kagan Publishing • 1 (800) 933-2667 • www.KaganOnline.com

Making Words (o, u, c, d, l, s)
Student Form

Instructions: Make one copy per student. Cut apart letters to use during
Activity 1: Making Words. Cut apart boxes after words are added for Activity 2: Sorting.

s						
l						
d						
c						
u						
o						

Lesson 2: "Jumping"
Activity 1: Making Words

The steps for this activity are the same as Lesson 1, Activity 1, but substitute the following words to make from the letters in jumping.

Words to Make from *Jumping*

Directions	Word	Teaching Point
Make: *up*	up	
Make: *in*	in	
Add a *p* to the beginning of the word.	pin	Discuss /in/ letter pattern.
Change the ending letter to a *g*.	pig	Stretch through the word to check it.
Replace the beginning letter with another consonant. Stretch through the word to make sure it's a real word.	jig	Stretch through the word together. Model how to say the word... /j/ /ig/ jig
Replace the *i* with a *u*.	jug	Stretch through the word together. Model how to say the word... /j/ /ug/ jug
Replace the *j* with an *m*.	mug	Have the students practice stretching through the word.
Switch the beginning and ending letters to form a new word.	gum	
Replace the *m* with another consonant to make a new word.	gun	
Make: *jump*	jump	Discuss /ump/ letter pattern.
Use all the letters to make the magic word.	jumping	Discuss covering up the '*ing*' and saying the word and then adding the ending back on. Practice.

Balanced Literacy • First Grade • Skidmore & Graber
Kagan Publishing • 1 (800) 933-2667 • www.KaganOnline.com

Activity 2: Sorting

The steps for this activity are the same as Lesson 1, Activity 2. Below is an example for Find My Rule using the jumping words and additional ideas for Find My Rule.

Ideas for Rules

- /ug/ word patterns
- /up/ word patterns
- /in/ word pattern
- words that start the same
- words that end the same
- short /u/
- short /i/

My Rule	Not My Rule
pig	jump
jig	

Example: /ig/ letter pattern

Activity 3: Transfer

The steps for this activity are the same as Lesson 1, Activity 3, except use the following words to spell.

Using What You Know
If you can spell... then you can spell....

pin	tin, win, fin, grin, chin, spin, thin
pig	dig, wig, twig, fig
mug	tug, rug, plug, snug, hug, bug, dug
gum	drum, hum, strum, chum
jump	bump, lump, stump, dump, hump

Making Words (*Jumping*)
Teacher Transparency Form

Instructions: Make a transparency of this page. Cut out letters and words to use during Activity 1: Making Words and with Activity 2: Sorting.

p	pig	gum				
m n	pin	mug	jumping			
j g	in	jug	jump			
i u	up	jig	gun			

Making Words (i, u, g, j, m, n, p)
Student Form

Instructions: Make one copy per student. Cut apart letters to use during Activity 1: Making Words. Cut apart boxes after words are added for Activity 2: Sorting.

p

n

m

j

g

u

i

Lesson 3: "Peanuts"
Activity 1: Making Words

The steps for this activity are the same as Lesson 1, Activity 1, but substitute the following words to make from the letters in peanuts.

Words to Make from *Peanuts*

Directions	Word	Teaching Point
Make: *us*	us	
Change the vowel and make '*as*'.	as	
Replace the ending letter '*s*' with an '*n*'.	an	
Add a '*t*' to the beginning of '*an*'.	tan	Discuss using the /an/ letter pattern to decode/write. Practice decoding: /t/ /an/; stretch through with finger and say it as a letter pattern.
Replace the '*t*' with a '*p*' to make a new word.	pan	Practice saying the word with the letter pattern.
Replace the ending letter with a different letter.	pat	Discuss /at/ letter pattern.
Rearrange the beginning letter and the ending letter to make a new word.	tap	Discuss /ap/ letter pattern. Practice checking the word.
Make: *sat*	sat	What letter pattern helped you?
Replace the vowel '*a*' with another vowel.	set	Discuss /et/ letter pattern.
Make: *pet*	pet	
Use a different beginning letter	net	
Replace the vowel '*e*' with a '*u*'.	nut	
Make: *ant* The black ant is climbing on my leg.	ant	The letter pattern /an/ is at the beginning of the word.
Add a beginning letter to make a word.	pant	Letter pattern /an/ is in the middle. Practice stretching through it.
Make: *pets*	pets	What letter pattern helped you?
Use the same letters and make '*step*'.	step	
Use the same letters and make '*pest*'.	pest	Discuss /est/ letter pattern.

Balanced Literacy • First Grade • Skidmore & Graber
Kagan Publishing • 1 (800) 933-2667 • www.KaganOnline.com

Words to Make from "Peanuts" (continued)

Directions	Word	Teaching Point
Replace the *e* with an *a*.	past	Slide through to check together.
Make: *neat*	neat	Discuss /ea/ letter pattern.
Replace the beginning letter with a different consonant.	seat	
Rearrange the letters and make '*east*.'	east	Letter /ea/ pattern is at the beginning.
Make: *tap*	tap	
Add a silent *e* to the end.	tape	Discuss the long vowel sound.
Make: *upset*	upset	Discuss compound words.
Use all the letters to make the magic word.	peanuts	Discuss letter patterns. Discuss compound words.

Activity 2: Sorting

The steps for this activity are the same as Lesson 1, Activity 2. Below is an example for Find My Rule using the peanuts *words and additional ideas for Find My Rule.*

Ideas for Rules

- /at/, /an/, /et/, /eat/ word patterns
- three-letter words
- four-letter words
- compound words
- short /a/
- short /e/

My Rule	Not My Rule
pan	loud
pat	
tap	

Example: short /a/ letter pattern

Activity 3: Transfer

The steps for this activity are the same as Lesson 1, Activity 3, except use the following words to spell.

Using What You Know

If you can spell...	Then you can spell...
ant	plant, chant
neat	heat, meat, treat, wheat
tape	cape, shape
past	last, fast, cast, blast

Making Words (*Peanuts*)
Teacher Transparency Form

Instructions: Make a transparency of this page. Cut out letters and words to use during Activity 1: Making Words and with Activity 2: Sorting.

t	tan	sat	nut	step	seat	peanuts
s	an	tap	net	pets	neat	upset
p						
u	as	pat	pet	pant	past	tape
n						
e	us	pan	set	ant	pest	east
a						

Balanced Literacy • First Grade • Skidmore & Graber
Kagan Publishing • 1 (800) 933-2667 • www.KaganOnline.com

Making Words (a, e, u, n, p, s, t)
Student Form

Instructions: Make one copy per student. Cut apart letters to use during Activity 1: Making Words.
Cut apart boxes after words are added for Activity 2: Sorting.

t

p s

u n

a e

Find My Rule Mat
for Making Words

Instructions: Make a transparency of this mat for Activity 2: Sorting. Make copies for each pair of students for Activity 2: Sorting.

My Rule	Not My Rule

Making Words Planning Form

Letters: _____

Magic Word: _____

Part I: Making Words (RallyTable)

Instructions: Use this planning form to create additional Making Words lessons.

Directions	Word	Teaching Point

Part 2: Sorting (Find My Rule)	Sort For:

Part 3: Transfer (RallyCoach)	Using What You Know

Making Words
Student Form

Instructions: Use this planning form to create the letters and words for additional Making Words lessons.

Who Knows?

Students mix about the room, finding others who can help them fill out their Find Someone Who word study worksheets.

STRUCTURE

Find Someone Who

Activity Steps

1. Every student receives a Find Someone Who worksheet.

2. Students mix around the room until they find a partner.

3. In pairs, Partner A asks a question from the worksheet; Partner B responds. Partner A records the answer on his or her worksheet.

4. Partner B checks and initials the answer.

5. Partner B asks a question. Partner A responds. Partner B records the answer on his or her worksheet.

6. Partner A checks and initials the answer.

7. Partners shake hands, part, and raise a hand again as they search for a new partner.

8. Students repeat the process until they complete their worksheets.

9. When their worksheets are completed, students sit down; seated students may be approached by others as a resource.

10. In teams, students compare answers; if there is disagreement or uncertainty, they raise four hands to ask a team question.

Blacklines

Rhyming Words, Word Family (_at), Endings, Vowels

Find Someone Who

Name _____

Instructions: Copy one page per student.

Rhyming Words, Word Family (_at), Endings, Vowels

Match Rhyming Words

rock •   • jar
frog •   • sock
car •   • dog

Initials

Rhyming Words, Word Family (_at), Endings, Vowels

Circle the Endings

jumps   jumped   jumping

Initials

Rhyming Words, Word Family (_at), Endings, Vowels

Circle the Vowels

a   t   s   o
p   y   i   m
e   c   u   h

Initials

Rhyming Words, Word Family (_at), Endings, Vowels

Add to the Word Family

<u>b</u>at

<u>s</u>at

_____

_____

Initials

Rhyming Words, Word Family (_at), Endings, Vowels

Add a Vowel

<u>a</u> or <u>o</u>

st_p

c_mp

sl_m

Initials

Adding Onsets, Adding -ed, -ing, Correct Spelling, Compound Words, Word Parts

Find Someone Who

Name _____

Instructions: Copy one page per student.

Adding Onsets, Adding -ed, -ing, Correct Spelling, Compound Words, Word Parts

Match

k •   • _ank

j •   • _ick

dr •   • _ump

Initials

Adding Onsets, Adding -ed, -ing, Correct Spelling, Compound Words, Word Parts

Add -ed or -ing

camp_____

bump_____

lick____

Initials

Adding Onsets, Adding -ed, -ing, Correct Spelling, Compound Words, Word Parts

Which word is not spelled right?

I wus going to the park to play.

Initials

Adding Onsets, Adding -ed, -ing, Correct Spelling, Compound Words, Word Parts

Say word. Clap.
How many word parts?

_____

_____

_____

_____

Initials

Adding Onsets, Adding -ed, -ing, Correct Spelling, Compound Words, Word Parts

Match to make compound words.

sun •   • corn

cup •   • set

pop •   • cake

Initials

Rhyming Words, ch/sh/th, Compound Words, Rhyming Words, Plurals

Find Someone Who

Name _____

Instructions: Copy one page per student.

Rhyming Words, ch/sh/th, Compound Words, Rhyming Words, Plurals

Match Rhyming Words

• •

• •

• •

Initials

Rhyming Words, ch/sh/th, Compound Words, Rhyming Words, Plurals

Add ch, sh, or th

fla_____

tee_____

lun_____

Initials

Rhyming Words, ch/sh/th, Compound Words, Rhyming Words, Plurals

Make Compound Words

| star | sun | corn | set | pop | fish |

_____   _____   _____

Initials

Rhyming Words, ch/sh/th, Compound Words, Rhyming Words, Plurals

Circle the Words That Rhyme With

thick   sick   sunk

clock   click   trick

thank   pick   slick

Initials

Rhyming Words, ch/sh/th, Compound Words, Rhyming Words, Plurals

Make Plurals

one bird ⟶ three _____

one duck ⟶ two _____

one ring ⟶ six _____

Initials

Find Someone Who Form

Name _____

Instructions: Use this form to create questions for additional activities.

Initials

Initials

Initials

Initials

Initials

Initials

Initials

Activity

Partner Word Study Practice

To practice word parts, rhyming words, and onsets/rimes, students quiz a partner, get quizzed by a partner, and then trade cards to repeat the process with a new partner.

Activity Steps

1. Each student receives a card with a question on the front and answer on the back.

2. All students stand up, put a hand up, and pair up.

3. Partner A quizzes Partner B.

4. Partner B answers.

5. Partner A checks the answer on back and praises or coaches.

6. Partners switch roles and quiz again.

7. After they have quizzed both ways, partners trade cards, and raise their hands to find a new partner. The partner quizzing and trading proceeds for numerous pairings.

STRUCTURE

Quiz-Quiz-Trade

Blacklines

Word Parts
Quiz-Quiz-Trade

Instructions: Copy enough cards so each student has one card. Cut on dotted lines and fold in half.

Word Parts	Word Parts
Say the word. Clap the parts. Do the words have the same number of parts? 	Answer:  yes

Word Parts	Word Parts
Say the word. Clap the parts. Do the words have the same number of parts? 	Answer:  no

Word Parts	Word Parts
Say the word. Clap the parts. Do the words have the same number of parts?  	Answer:  no

Word Parts	Word Parts
Say the word. Clap the parts. Do the words have the same number of parts? 	Answer:  yes

Word Parts
Quiz-Quiz-Trade

Instructions: Copy enough cards so each student has one card. Cut on dotted lines and fold in half.

Word Parts	Word Parts
Say the word. Clap the parts. Do the words have the same number of parts? 	Answer: 
Word Parts	Word Parts
Say the word. Clap the parts. Do the words have the same number of parts?  	Answer: 
Word Parts	Word Parts
Say the word. Clap the parts. Do the words have the same number of parts?  	Answer: 
Word Parts	Word Parts
Say the word. Clap the parts. Do the words have the same number of parts? 	Answer: 

Word Parts
Quiz-Quiz-Trade

Instructions: Copy enough cards so each student has one card. Cut on dotted lines and fold in half.

Word Parts	Word Parts
Say the word. Clap the parts. Do the words have the same number of parts?	Answer: **yes** 

Word Parts	Word Parts
Say the word. Clap the parts. Do the words have the same number of parts?	Answer: **yes** 

Word Parts	Word Parts
Say the word. Clap the parts. Do the words have the same number of parts? 	Answer: **yes** 

Word Parts	Word Parts
Say the word. Clap the parts. Do the words have the same number of parts? 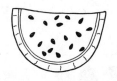	Answer: **yes** 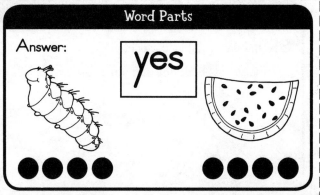

Word Parts
Quiz-Quiz-Trade

Instructions: Copy enough cards so each student has one card. Cut on dotted lines and fold in half.

Word Parts	Word Parts
Say the word. Clap the parts. Do the words have the same number of parts?	Answer: **yes**

Word Parts	Word Parts
Say the word. Clap the parts. Do the words have the same number of parts?	Answer: **no**

Word Parts	Word Parts
Say the word. Clap the parts. Do the words have the same number of parts?	Answer: **no**

Word Parts	Word Parts
Say the word. Clap the parts. Do the words have the same number of parts?	Answer: **yes**

Word Parts
Quiz-Quiz-Trade

Instructions: Copy enough cards so each student has one card. Cut on dotted lines and fold in half.

Word Parts	Word Parts
Say the word. Clap the parts. Do the words have the same number of parts? 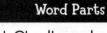	Answer:  **yes**
Say the word. Clap the parts. Do the words have the same number of parts? 	Answer: **no** 
Say the word. Clap the parts. Do the words have the same number of parts? 	Answer: **no** 
Say the word. Clap the parts. Do the words have the same number of parts?  	Answer:  **no**

Word Parts
Quiz-Quiz-Trade

Instructions: Copy enough cards so each student has one card. Cut on dotted lines and fold in half.

Word Parts
Say the word. Clap the parts.
Do the words have the same number of parts?

Word Parts
Answer: **yes**

Word Parts
Say the word. Clap the parts.
Do the words have the same number of parts?

Word Parts
Answer: **no**

Word Parts
Say the word. Clap the parts.
Do the words have the same number of parts?

Word Parts
Answer: **no**

Word Parts
Say the word. Clap the parts.
Do the words have the same number of parts?

Word Parts
Answer: **no**

Word Parts
Quiz-Quiz-Trade

Instructions: Copy enough cards so each student has one card. Cut on dotted lines and fold in half.

Word Parts	Word Parts
Say the word. Clap the parts. Do the words have the same number of parts?	Answer: **no** 
Say the word. Clap the parts. Do the words have the same number of parts? 	Answer: **yes** 
Say the word. Clap the parts. Do the words have the same number of parts? 	Answer: **yes** 
Say the word. Clap the parts. Do the words have the same number of parts? 	Answer: **no** 

Rhyming Words
Quiz-Quiz-Trade

Instructions: Copy enough cards so each student has one card. Cut on dotted lines and fold in half.

Rhyming Words	Rhyming Words
Rhyming Words? 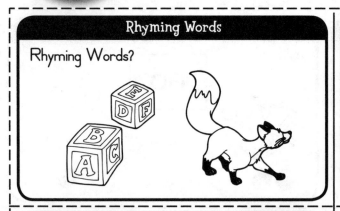	Answer: **yes** (blocks, fox)
Rhyming Words? 	Answer: **yes** (door, four)
Rhyming Words? 	Answer: **no** (knot, coat)
Rhyming Words? 	Answer: **no** (mask, skunk)

Balanced Literacy • First Grade • Skidmore & Graber
Kagan Publishing • 1 (800) 933-2667 • www.KaganOnline.com

Rhyming Words
Quiz-Quiz-Trade

Instructions: Copy enough cards so each student has one card. Cut on dotted lines and fold in half.

Rhyming Words	Rhyming Words
Rhyming Words? 	Answer: **no** (ant, dart)
Rhyming Words	Rhyming Words
Rhyming Words? 	Answer: **no** (train, lion)
Rhyming Words	Rhyming Words
Rhyming Words? 	Answer: **yes** (car, jar)
Rhyming Words	Rhyming Words
Rhyming Words? 	Answer: **yes** (paw, saw)

Rhyming Words
Quiz-Quiz-Trade

Instructions: Copy enough cards so each student has one card. Cut on dotted lines and fold in half.

Rhyming Words	Rhyming Words
Rhyming Words? 	Answer: **yes** (frog, dog)
Rhyming Words? 	Answer: **no** (globe, tub)
Rhyming Words? 	Answer: **no** (nose, bus)
Rhyming Words? 	Answer: **yes** (rain, chain)

Rhyming Words
Quiz-Quiz-Trade

Instructions: Copy enough cards so each student has one card. Cut on dotted lines and fold in half.

Rhyming Words	Rhyming Words
Rhyming Words? 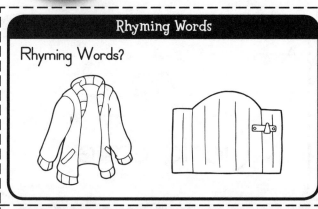	Answer: **no** (coat, gate)
Rhyming Words? 	Answer: **yes** (lake, rake)
Rhyming Words? 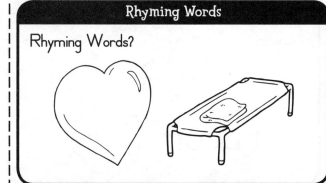	Answer: **no** (heart, cot)
Rhyming Words? 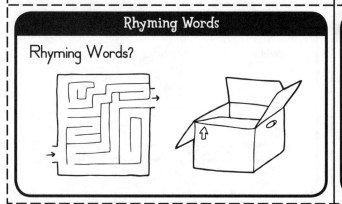	Answer: **no** (maze, box)

Rhyming Words
Quiz-Quiz-Trade

Instructions: Copy enough cards so each student has one card. Cut on dotted lines and fold in half.

Rhyming Words	Rhyming Words
Rhyming Words? 	Answer: **no** (lock, cake)
Rhyming Words Rhyming Words? 	Rhyming Words Answer: **yes** (skate, gate)
Rhyming Words Rhyming Words? 	Rhyming Words Answer: **no** (bear, fire)
Rhyming Words Rhyming Words? 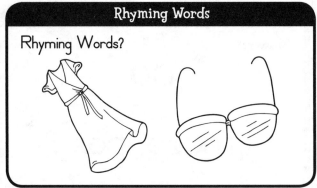	Rhyming Words Answer: **no** (dress, glasses)

Balanced Literacy • First Grade • Skidmore & Graber
Kagan Publishing • 1 (800) 933-2667 • www.KaganOnline.com

Rhyming Words
Quiz-Quiz-Trade

Instructions: Copy enough cards so each student has one card. Cut on dotted lines and fold in half.

Rhyming Words	Rhyming Words
Rhyming Words? 	Answer: **yes** (rock, sock) 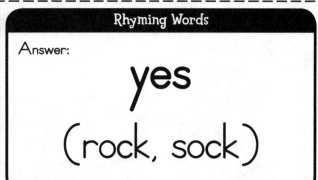
Rhyming Words? 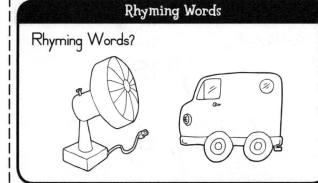	Answer: **yes** (fan, van) 
Rhyming Words? 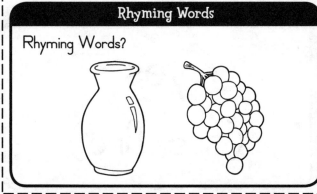	Answer: **no** (vase, grapes) 
Rhyming Words? 	Answer: **yes** (nail, whale) 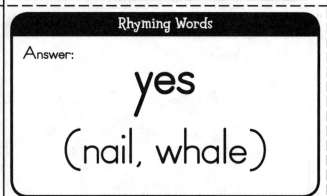

Rhyming Words
Quiz-Quiz-Trade

Instructions: Copy enough cards so each student has one card. Cut on dotted lines and fold in half.

Rhyming Words	Rhyming Words
Rhyming Words? 	Answer: **yes** (vest, nest)
Rhyming Words	Rhyming Words
Rhyming Words? 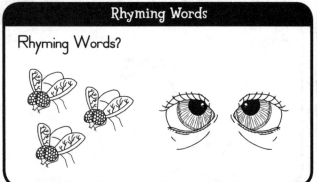	Answer: **yes** (flies, eyes)
Rhyming Words	Rhyming Words
Rhyming Words? 	Answer: **yes** (tire, fire)
Rhyming Words	Rhyming Words
Rhyming Words? 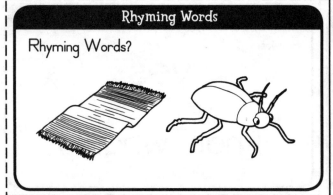	Answer: **yes** (rug, bug)

Balanced Literacy • First Grade • Skidmore & Graber
Kagan Publishing • 1 (800) 933-2667 • www.KaganOnline.com

Onsets and Rimes
Quiz-Quiz-Trade

Instructions: Copy enough cards so each student has one card. Cut on dotted lines and fold in half.

Onsets and Rimes	Onsets and Rimes
Read these. Which is a word?	Answer:
stop	stop
frop	

Onsets and Rimes	Onsets and Rimes
Read these. Which is a word?	Answer:
brip	drip
drip	

Onsets and Rimes	Onsets and Rimes
Read these. Which is a word?	Answer:
frill	frill
plill	

Onsets and Rimes	Onsets and Rimes
Read these. Which is a word?	Answer:
flash	flash
plash	

Onsets and Rimes
Quiz-Quiz-Trade

Instructions: Copy enough cards so each student has one card. Cut on dotted lines and fold in half.

Onsets and Rimes	Onsets and Rimes
Read these. Which is a word?	Answer:
frip	trip
trip	

Onsets and Rimes	Onsets and Rimes
Read these. Which is a word?	Answer:
grin	grin
glin	

Onsets and Rimes	Onsets and Rimes
Read these. Which is a word?	Answer:
trot	trot
prot	

Onsets and Rimes	Onsets and Rimes
Read these. Which is a word?	Answer:
trank	blank
blank	

Balanced Literacy • First Grade • Skidmore & Graber
Kagan Publishing • 1 (800) 933-2667 • www.KaganOnline.com

Onsets and Rimes
Quiz-Quiz-Trade

Instructions: Copy enough cards so each student has one card. Cut on dotted lines and fold in half.

Onsets and Rimes	Onsets and Rimes
Read these. Which is a word? stack drack	Answer: stack
Read these. Which is a word? black prack	Answer: black
Read these. Which is a word? plill still	Answer: still
Read these. Which is a word? stap trap	Answer: trap

Onsets and Rimes
Quiz-Quiz-Trade

Instructions: Copy enough cards so each student has one card. Cut on dotted lines and fold in half.

Onsets and Rimes	Onsets and Rimes
Read these. Which is a word?	Answer:
drink	drink
prink	

Onsets and Rimes	Onsets and Rimes
Read these. Which is a word?	Answer:
blan	plan
plan	

Onsets and Rimes	Onsets and Rimes
Read these. Which is a word?	Answer:
clap	clap
frap	

Onsets and Rimes	Onsets and Rimes
Read these. Which is a word?	Answer:
flot	slot
slot	

Onsets and Rimes
Quiz-Quiz-Trade

Instructions: Copy enough cards so each student has one card. Cut on dotted lines and fold in half.

Onsets and Rimes	Onsets and Rimes
Read these. Which is a word? prash crash	Answer: crash
Onsets and Rimes	Onsets and Rimes
Read these. Which is a word? flat grat	Answer: flat
Onsets and Rimes	Onsets and Rimes
Read these. Which is a word? drock clock	Answer: clock
Onsets and Rimes	Onsets and Rimes
Read these. Which is a word? block grock	Answer: block

Onsets and Rimes
Quiz-Quiz-Trade

Instructions: Copy enough cards so each student has one card. Cut on dotted lines and fold in half.

Onsets and Rimes	Onsets and Rimes
Read these. Which is a word? stick grick	Answer: stick
Read these. Which is a word? blick brick	Answer: brick
Read these. Which is a word? bruck truck	Answer: truck
Read these. Which is a word? bring tring	Answer: bring

Balanced Literacy • First Grade • Skidmore & Graber
Kagan Publishing • 1 (800) 933-2667 • www.KaganOnline.com

Onsets and Rimes
Quiz-Quiz-Trade

Instructions: Copy enough cards so each student has one card. Cut on dotted lines and fold in half.

Onsets and Rimes	Onsets and Rimes
Read these. Which is a word? prug plug	Answer: plug
Read these. Which is a word? stay dray	Answer: stay
Read these. Which is a word? drit slit	Answer: slit
Read these. Which is a word? grill glill	Answer: grill

Coach Me

Four different types of word study RallyCoach activities are provided: 1) cube, 2) spinner, 3) word cards, and 4) sorting mat. Using the materials provided, one partner completes the task while the other is the coach. They switch roles for each new problem.

Activity Steps

1. Depending on the activity below, each pair receives either a cube and a worksheet, a spinner and a worksheet, word cards, or a sorting mat and word cards.

2. First Partner A completes the task.
   - Cube(s): Partner rolls cube(s) and uses result to fill in worksheet.
   - Spinner(s): Partner spins spinner(s) and uses result to fill in worksheet.
   - Word Cards and Letter Cards: Partner chooses a letter card to complete a word.
   - Word Cards: Partner chooses two words to make a compound word.
   - Word Cards: Partner decodes words using onset, rime or endings.
   - Sorting Mat: Partner picks a word card and sorts it on the mat.

3. Partner B watches and listens, checks, and praises.

4. Then, Partner B rolls the cube, spins the spinner, or selects the next word card. Partner B completes the next problem.

5. Partner A watches and listens, checks, and praises.

6. The process continues until they complete their worksheet or sort all word cards.

STRUCTURE

RallyCoach

Coach Me (continued)

Blacklines

Onset Cube (d, l, r, s, t, w)
(Use with _ay, _ip, _ell Rime Cube.)
RallyCoach

Instructions: Copy the cube pattern onto cardstock for each pair. Copy the onset cube and rime cube on different colors. Cut out, fold, and tape together to form a cube. Partners take turns rolling the cubes. The student rolling the cubes states the word made. If it is a real word, both partners write the word on their individual worksheets.

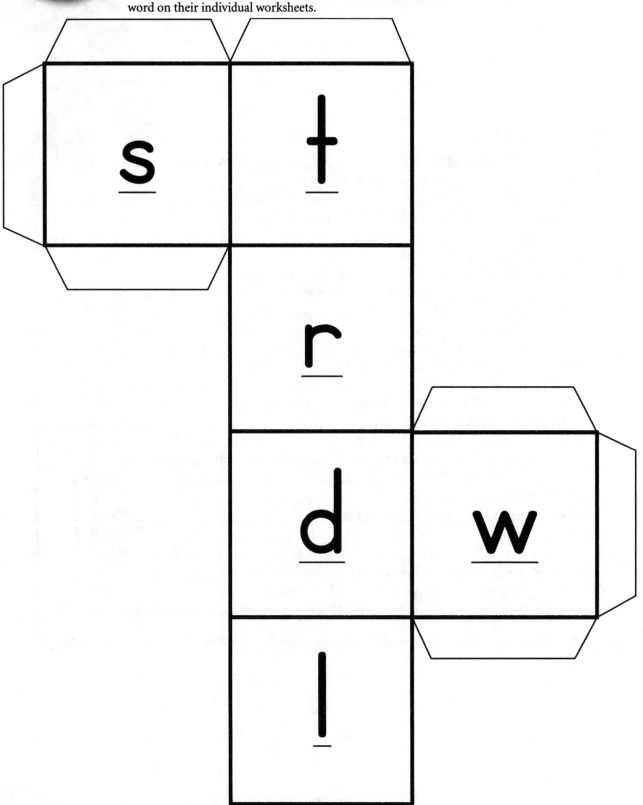

Rime Cube (_ay, _ip_ell)
(Use with d, l, r, s, t, w Onset Cube.)
RallyCoach

Instructions: Copy the cube pattern onto cardstock for each pair. Copy the onset cube and rime cube on different colors. Cut out, fold, and tape together to form a cube. Partners take turns rolling the cubes. The student rolling the cubes states the word made. If it is a real word, both partners write the word on their individual worksheets.

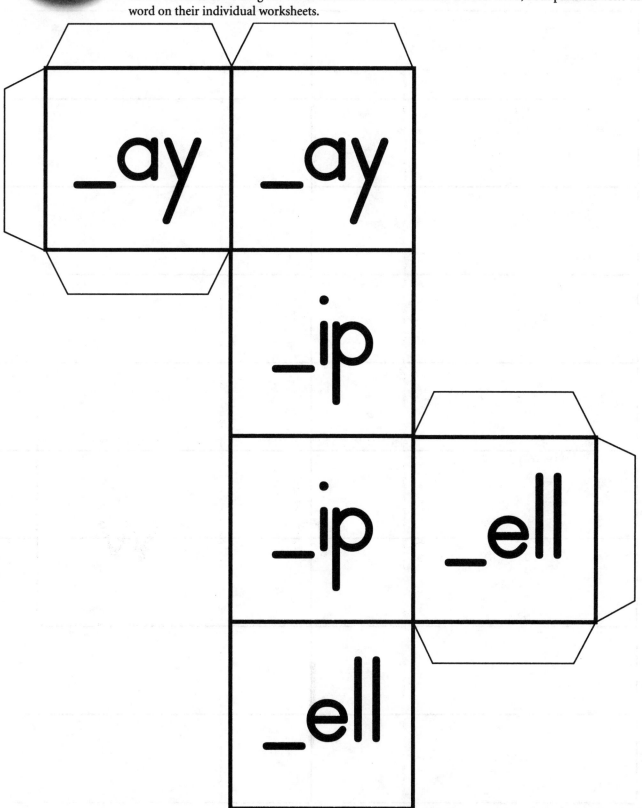

Onset and Rime Cubes Worksheet
RallyCoach

Instructions: Partners use worksheet with cubes.

Balanced Literacy • First Grade • Skidmore & Graber
Kagan Publishing • 1 (800) 933-2667 • www.KaganOnline.com

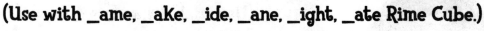

Onset Cube (f, l, m, r, s, t)
(Use with _ame, _ake, _ide, _ane, _ight, _ate Rime Cube.)
RallyCoach

Instructions: Copy the cube pattern onto cardstock for each pair. Copy the onset cube and rime cube on different colors. Cut out, fold, and tape together to form a cube. Partners take turns rolling the cube(s). The student rolling the cube(s) states the word made. If it is a real word, both partners write the word on their individual worksheets.

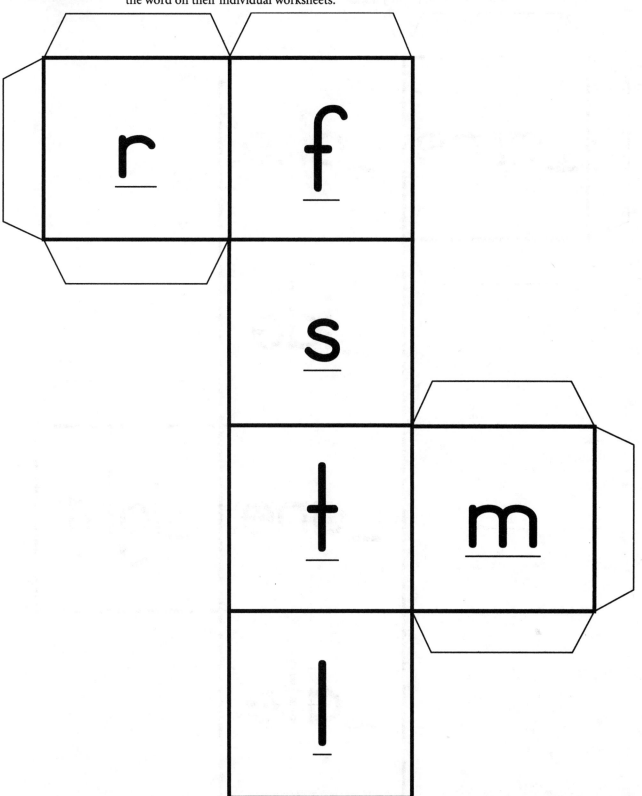

Long Vowel Rime Cube
(Use with f, l, m, r, s, t Onset Cube.)
RallyCoach

Instructions: Copy the cube pattern onto cardstock for each pair. Copy the onset cube and rime cube on different colors. Cut out, fold, and tape together to form a cube. Partners take turns rolling the cubes. The student rolling the cubes states the word made. If it is a real word, both partners write the word on their individual worksheets.

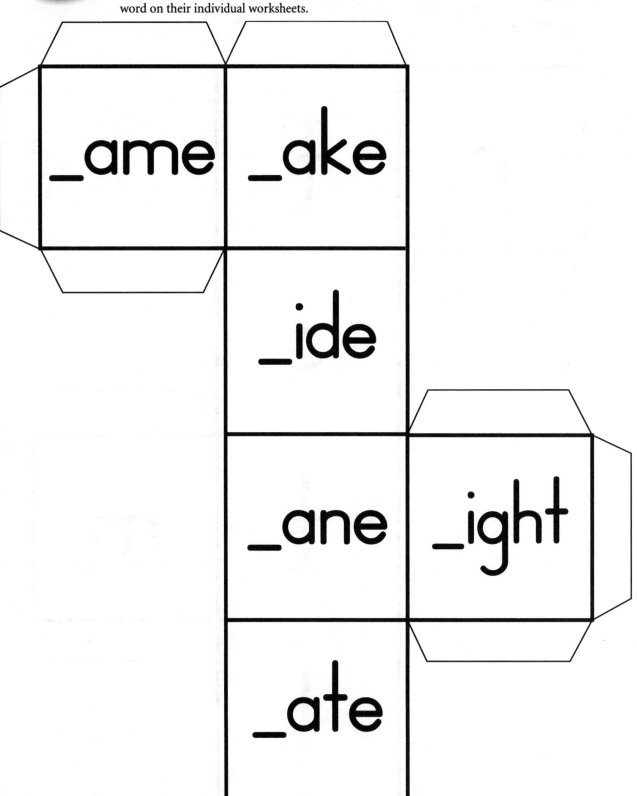

Balanced Literacy • First Grade • Skidmore & Graber
Kagan Publishing • 1 (800) 933-2667 • www.KaganOnline.com

Onset and Long Vowel
Rime Cubes Worksheet
RallyCoach

Instructions: Partners use worksheet with cubes.

Rime Cube (_ew and _y)
(Use with bl, cr, dr, fl, sl, st Onset Cube.)
RallyCoach

Instructions: Copy the cube pattern onto cardstock for each pair. Copy the onset cube and rime cube on different colors. Cut out, fold, and tape together to form a cube. Partners take turns rolling the cubes. The student rolling the cubes states the word made. If it is a real word, both partners write the word on their individual worksheets.

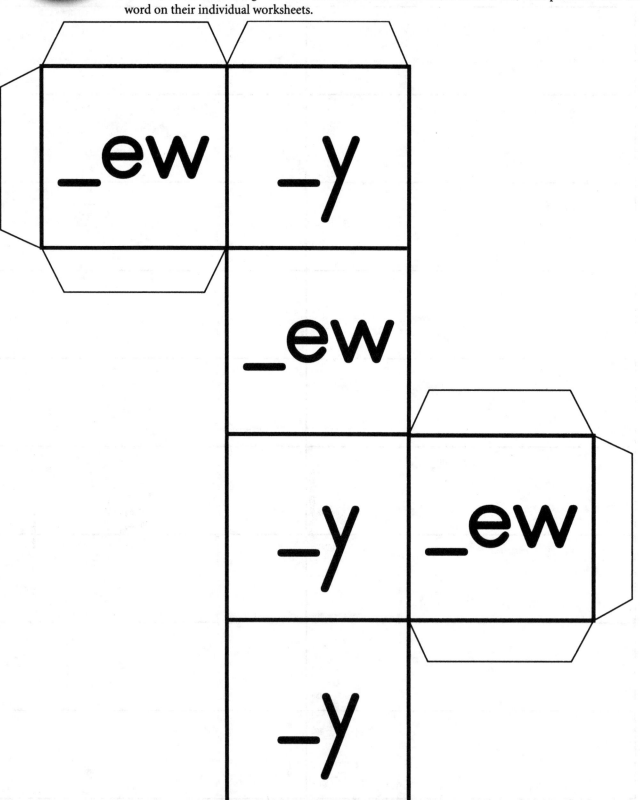

Balanced Literacy • First Grade • Skidmore & Graber
Kagan Publishing • 1 (800) 933-2667 • www.KaganOnline.com

Onset Blends Cube
(Use with _ew and _y Rime Cube.)
RallyCoach

Instructions: Copy the cube pattern onto cardstock for each pair. Copy the onset cube and rime cube on different colors. Cut out, fold, and tape together to form a cube. Partners take turns rolling the cubes. The student rolling the cubes states the word made. If it is a real word, both partners write the word on their individual worksheets.

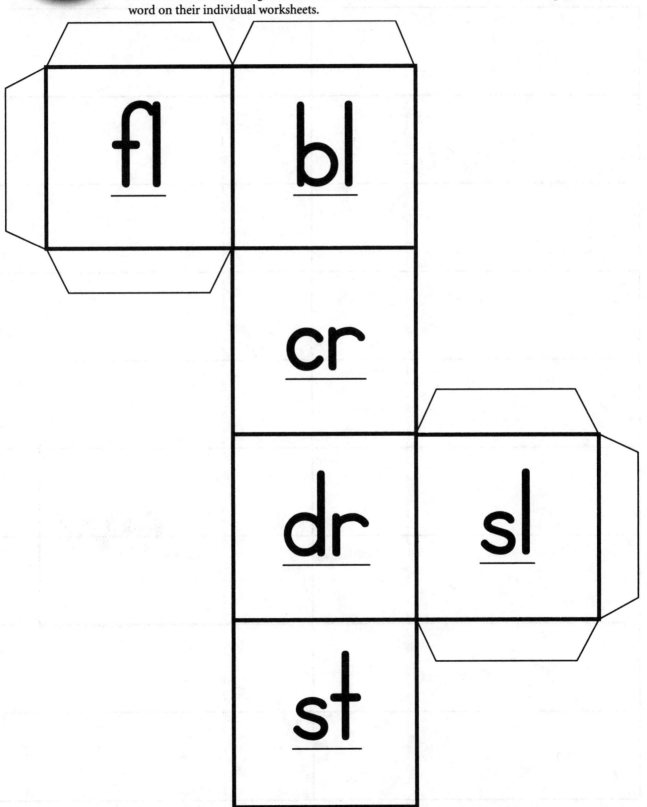

Onset Blend and Rime Cube Worksheet
RallyCoach

Instructions: Partners use worksheet with cubes.

Rime Cube
(Use with fl, tr, gr, dr, sk, pl Onset Cube.)
RallyCoach

Instructions: Copy the cube pattern onto cardstock for each pair. Copy the onset cube and rime cube on different colors. Cut out, fold, and tape together to form a cube. Partners take turns rolling the cubes. The student rolling the cubes states the word made. If it is a real word, both partners write the word on their individual worksheets.

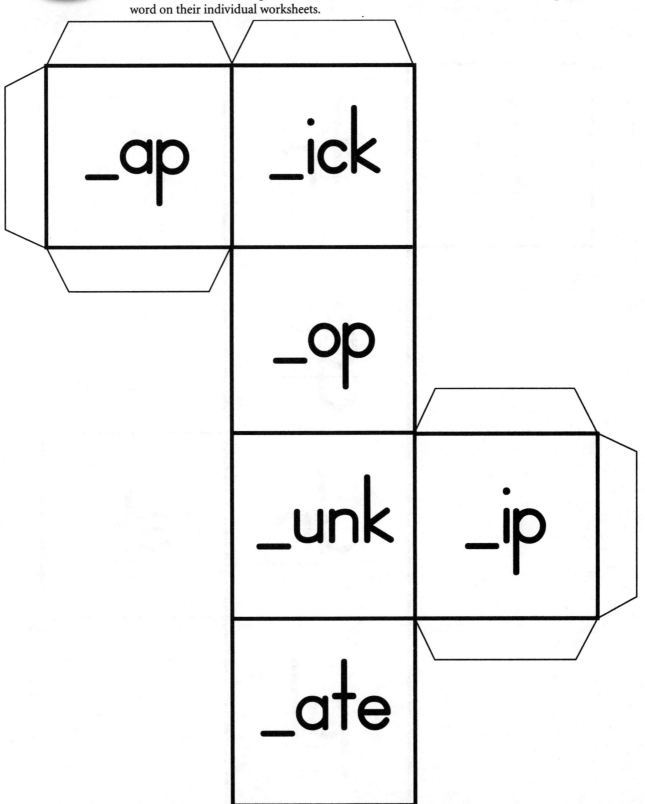

_ap

_ick

_op

_unk

_ip

_ate

Onset Blends Cube
(Use with _ap, _ick, _op, _unk, _ip, _ate Rime Cube.)
RallyCoach

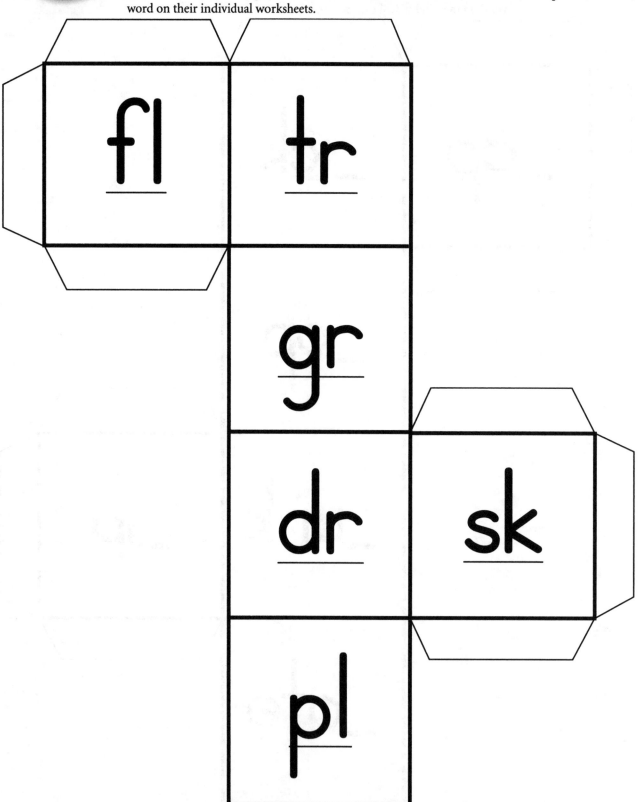

Instructions: Copy the cube pattern onto cardstock for each pair. Copy the onset cube and rime cube on different colors. Cut out, fold, and tape together to form a cube. Partners take turns rolling the cubes. The student rolling the cubes states the word made. If it is a real word, both partners write the word on their individual worksheets.

fl

tr

gr

dr   sk

pl

Onsets and Rime Worksheet
RallyCoach

Instructions: Partners use worksheet with cubes.

Adding Endings -ed, -ing Cube
RallyCoach

Instructions: Copy the cube pattern onto cardstock for each pair. Cut out, fold, and tape together to form a cube. Partners take turns rolling the cube. The student rolling the cube places the ending on a word on the worksheet and states the word.

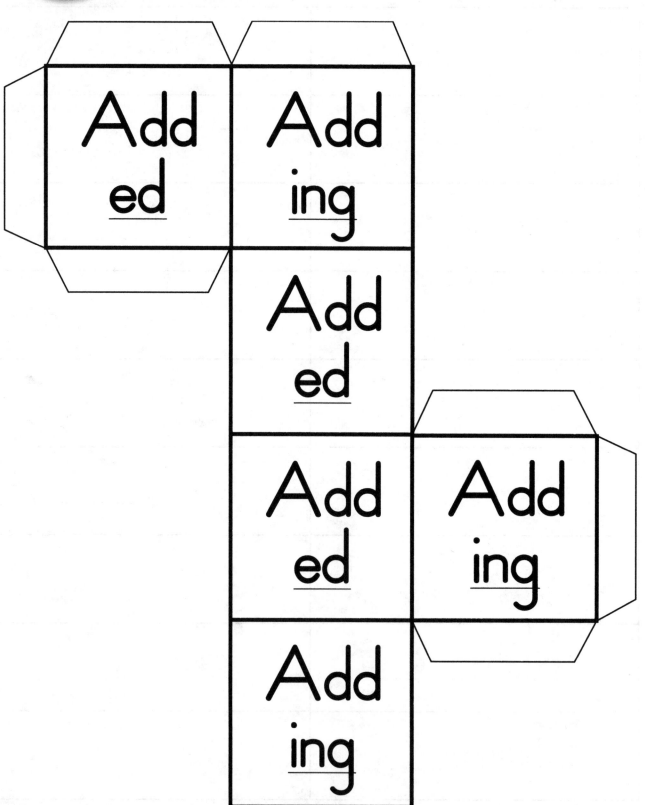

Endings (-ed, -ing) Worksheet
RallyCoach

Instructions: Partners use worksheet with Adding Endings (-ed, -ing) Cube. Student adds ending to a word on the worksheet, then reads the word.

pack_____	talk_____
grill_____	crack_____
dash_____	play_____
rain_____	jump_____
thank_____	spill_____
lick_____	trick_____
chill_____	pick_____
walk_____	snack_____
crawl_____	ask_____

Rime Spinner (_ack, _ick, and _ock)
RallyCoach

Instructions: Copy the spinner onto cardstock for each pair. Add a plastic/metal spinner in the middle or use a spinner made from a paper clip and a pencil. (To make a paper clip spinner: Place a paper clip over the center of the spinner. Place the pencil point on the center point of the spinner, through the paper clip. Using the other hand, spin the paper clip around the pencil point.) Partners take turns spinning. The student spinning chooses an incomplete word on the worksheet to form a word.

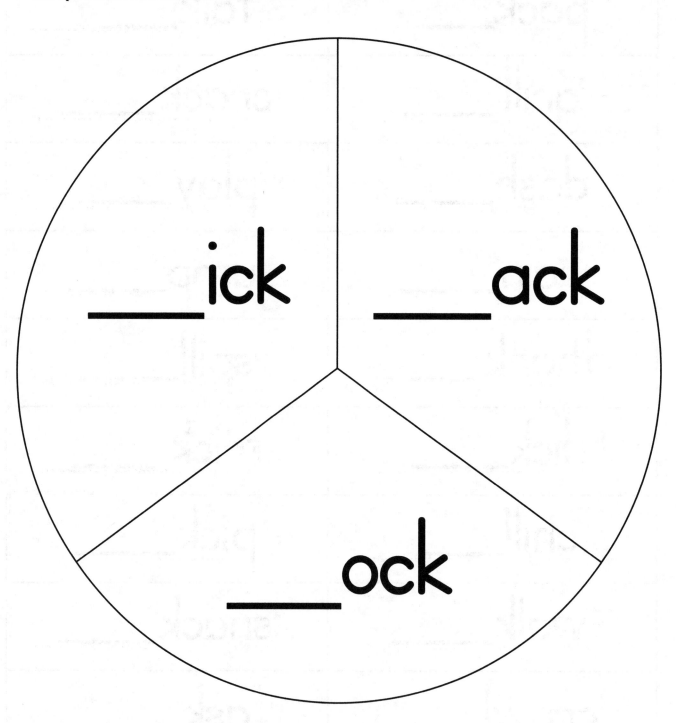

(_ack, _ick, and _ock) Worksheet

RallyCoach

Instructions: Partners use worksheet with Rime Spinner (_ack, _ick, _ock).

l_____	sn_____
th_____	st_____
sl_____	r_____
p_____	b_____
m_____	br_____
fl_____	cl_____
sh_____	k_____
s_____	tr_____
t_____	ch_____

Rime Spinner (_ay, _op, _ick, _ack, _ash)
(Use with Onset Spinner st, tr, pr.)
RallyCoach

Instructions: Copy the spinner(s) onto cardstock for each pair. Add a plastic/metal spinner in the middle or use a spinner made from a paper clip and a pencil. (To make a paper clip spinner: Place a paper clip over the center of the spinner. Place the pencil point on the center point of the spinner, through the paper clip. Using the other hand, spin the paper clip around the pencil point.) Partners take turns spinning both spinners. The student spinning states the word made. If it is a real word, both partners write the word on their individual worksheets.

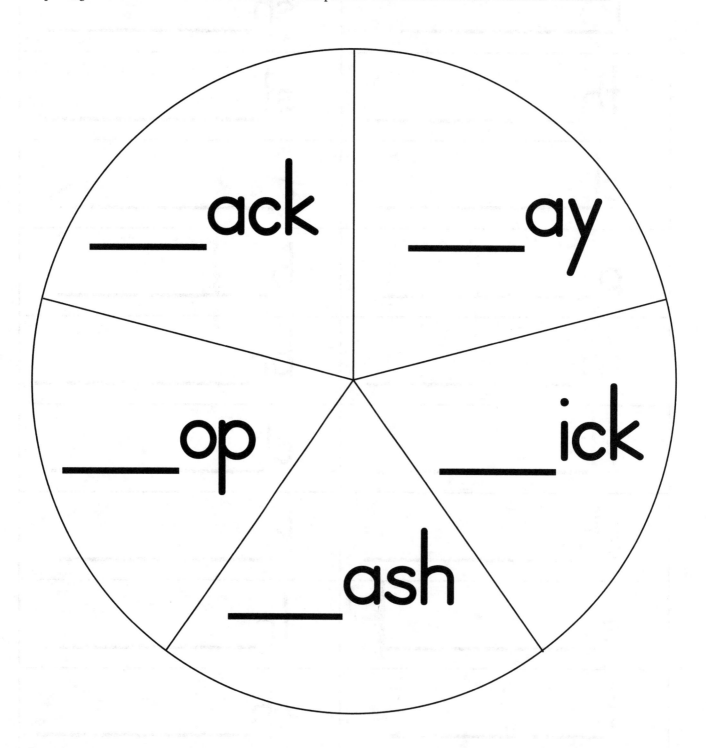

Onset Spinner (st, tr, pr)
(Use with Rime Spinner _ack, _ay, _op, _ick, _ash.)
RallyCoach

Instructions: Copy the spinner(s) onto cardstock for each pair. Add a plastic/metal spinner in the middle or use a spinner made from a paper clip and a pencil. (To make a paper clip spinner: Place a paper clip over the center of the spinner. Place the pencil point on the center point of the spinner, through the paper clip. Using the other hand, spin the paper clip around the pencil point.) Partners take turns spinning both spinners. The student spinning states the word made. If it is a real word, both partners write the word on their individual worksheets.

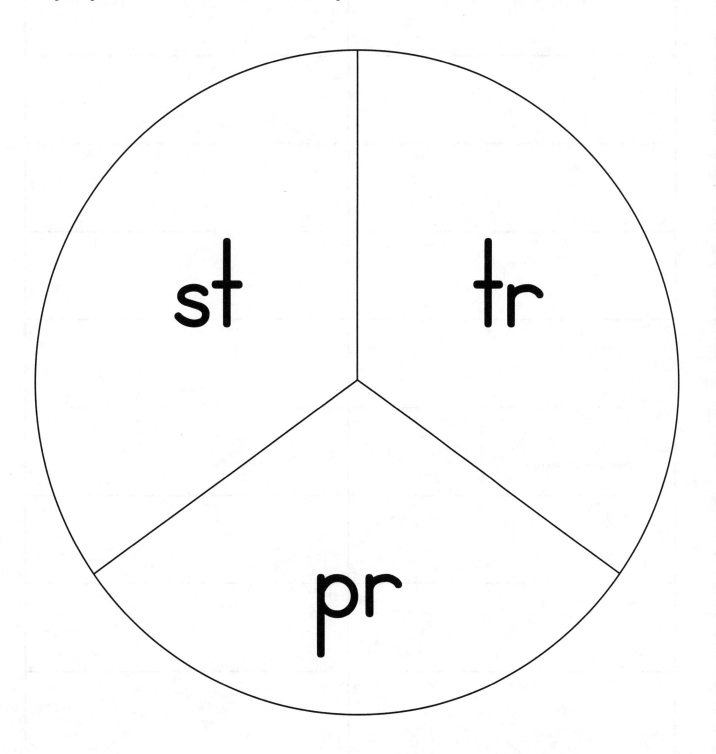

Onset and Rime Spinners Worksheet
RallyCoach

Instructions: Partners use worksheet with Onset and Rime Spinners (-ack, -ash, -ay, -ick, -op).

Balanced Literacy • First Grade • Skidmore & Graber
Kagan Publishing • 1 (800) 933-2667 • www.KaganOnline.com

 WORD STUDY
BlackLine

Word Cards and Vowel Cards #1
(Adding Medial Vowels)
RallyCoach

Instructions: Partners take turns placing letter cards in the blanks to make words. The words are written on the worksheet.

c __ t	f __ t
c __ p	v __ n
c __ n	g __ t
m __ n	l __ t

a e i o u

Word Cards and Vowel Cards #2
(Adding Medial Vowels)
RallyCoach

Instructions: Partners take turns placing letter cards in the blanks to make words. The words are written on the worksheet.

d___sh	fl___p
sh___p	th___nk
tr___ck	ch__mp
st_mp	st___ck

a	e	i	o	u

Adding Medial Vowels Worksheet
RallyCoach

Instructions: Use the spaces below to write the words made with the word cards and vowel cards.

Word Cards and Vowel Cards #1
(Adding Medial Vowels and Silent e)
RallyCoach

Instructions: Partners take turns placing letter cards in the blanks to make words. Words may be made with and without the silent "e" on the end. The words are written on the worksheet.

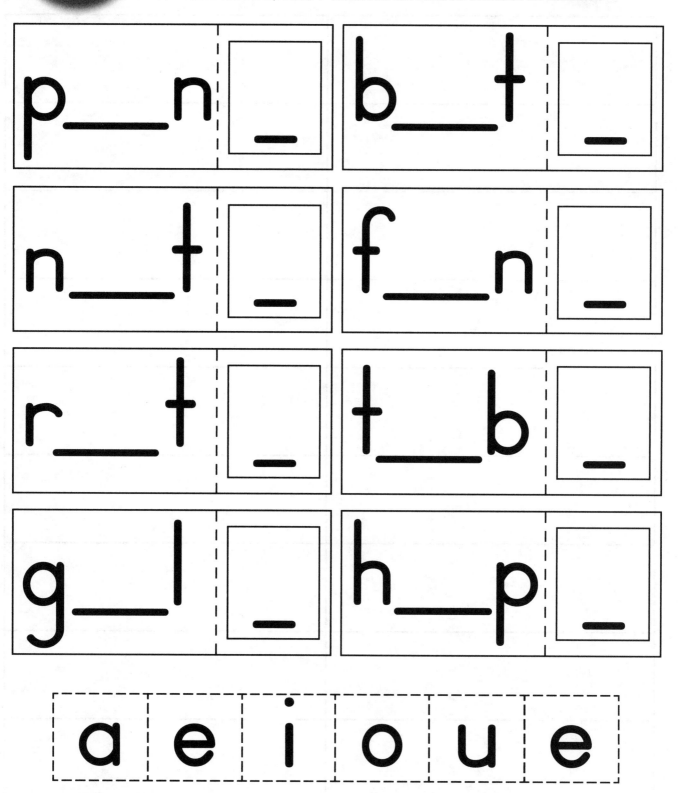

Word Cards and Vowel Cards #2
(Adding Medial Vowels and Silent e)
RallyCoach

Instructions: Partners take turns placing letter cards in the blanks to make words. Words may be made with and without the silent "*e*" on the end. The words are written on the worksheet.

d_m   _

p_ _l   _

t_ _p   _

r_ _b   _

k_ _t   _

m_d   _

c_ _n   _

c_ _t   _

a e i o u e

Worksheet
(Adding Medial Vowels and Silent e)
RallyCoach

Instructions: Use the spaces below to write the words made with the word cards and vowel cards.

WORD STUDY Blackline

Onset Cards
(For _ack, _ill, _ay Rime Cards)
RallyCoach

Instructions: Partners take turns placing onset cards on the rime cards to make words.

Onset and Rime Cards: sp	Onset and Rime Cards: dr	Onset and Rime Cards: f	Onset and Rime Cards: m
Onset and Rime Cards: sh	Onset and Rime Cards: pr	Onset and Rime Cards: bl	Onset and Rime Cards: sw
Onset and Rime Cards: pl	Onset and Rime Cards: thr	Onset and Rime Cards: cl	Onset and Rime Cards: tr
Onset and Rime Cards: w	Onset and Rime Cards: d	Onset and Rime Cards: tr	Onset and Rime Cards: ch
Onset and Rime Cards: s	Onset and Rime Cards: cr	Onset and Rime Cards: qu	Onset and Rime Cards: sk
Onset and Rime Cards: sn	Onset and Rime Cards: l	Onset and Rime Cards: sw	Onset and Rime Cards: h

Rime Cards (_ack, _ill, _ay)
RallyCoach

Instructions: Partners take turns placing onset cards on the rime cards to make words. Cards on this page are for 2 pairs of students.

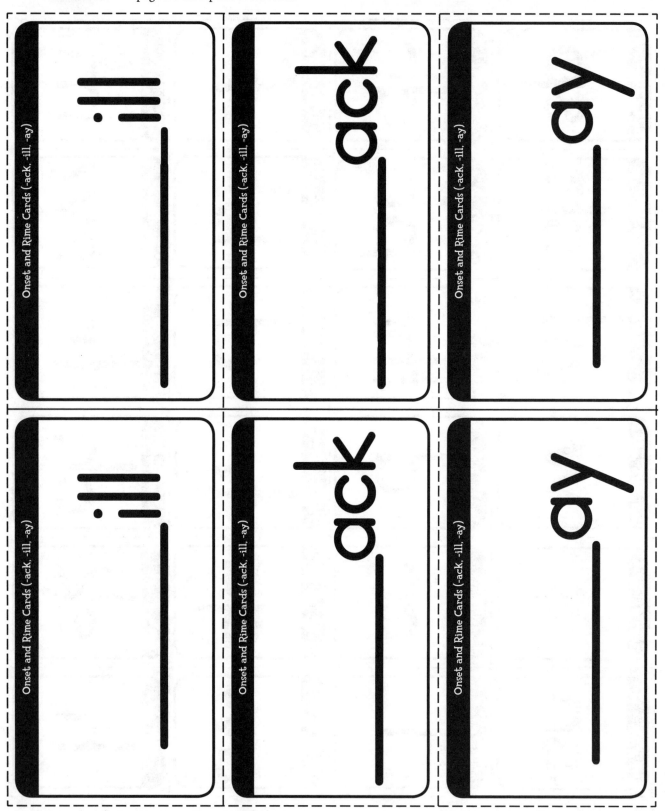

Letter Pattern Cards (_ew, _igh)
RallyCoach

Instructions: Partners take turns placing letter pattern cards on the word cards to make words. Copy these Letter Pattern Cards on a different color of paper than the Word Cards.

Letter Pattern Cards	Letter Pattern Cards	Letter Pattern Cards	Letter Pattern Cards	Letter Pattern Cards	Letter Pattern Cards
ew	igh	ew	igh	ew	igh
ew	igh	ew	igh	ew	igh
ew	igh	ew	igh	ew	igh
ew	igh	ew	igh	ew	igh
ew	igh	ew	igh	ew	igh
ew	igh	ew	igh	ew	igh

Word Cards #1 (ew, igh)

RallyCoach

Instructions: Partners take turns placing letter pattern cards on the word cards to make words.

bl____	h____
s____t	gr____
n____	fl____
f____	m____t
dr____	n____t

Word Cards #2 (ew, igh)
RallyCoach

Instructions: Partners take turns placing letter pattern cards on the word cards to make words.

l__t	d___
cr___	s___
r___t	scr___
fr___t	st___
ch___	t___t

Consonant Digraph Cards (sh, ch, th)
RallyCoach

Instructions: Partners take turns placing letter pattern cards on the word cards to make words. Copy these Letter Pattern Cards on a different color of paper than the Word Cards.

Digraph Cards	Digraph Cards	Digraph Cards	Digraph Cards	Digraph Cards	Digraph Cards
sh	ch	th	sh	ch	th
sh	ch	th	sh	ch	th
sh	ch	th	sh	ch	th
sh	ch	th	sh	ch	th
sh	ch	th	sh	ch	th
sh	ch	th	sh	ch	th

Word Cards #1 (sh, ch, th)
RallyCoach

Instructions: Partners take turns placing letter pattern cards on the word cards to make words.

fi___	___ime
___ank	cra___
___ell	___amp
___rink	tee___
___at	wi___

Word Cards #2 (sh, ch, th)
RallyCoach

Instructions: Partners take turns placing letter pattern cards on the word cards to make words.

__alk	__imp
fla__	spla__
tra__	ri__
lun__	__orn
__ark	crun__

 Balanced Literacy • First Grade • Skidmore & Graber
Kagan Publishing • 1 (800) 933-2667 • www.KaganOnline.com

Letter Pattern Cards (ar, ou)
RallyCoach

Instructions: Partners take turns placing letter pattern cards on the word cards to make words. Copy these Letter Pattern Cards on a different color of paper than the Word Cards.

Letter Pattern Cards	Letter Pattern Cards	Letter Pattern Cards	Letter Pattern Cards
ar	ou	ar	ou
ar	ou	ar	ou
ar	ou	ar	ou
ar	ou	ar	ou
ar	ou	ar	ou
ar	ou	ar	ou

Word Cards #1 (ar, ou)
RallyCoach

Instructions: Partners take turns placing letter pattern cards in the word card blanks to make words.

st___	sh___t
r___nd	f___m
d___k	p___k
___t	l___d
sh___k	c___ch

Balanced Literacy • First Grade • Skidmore & Graber
Kagan Publishing • 1 (800) 933-2667 • www.KaganOnline.com

Word Cards #2 (ar, ou)
RallyCoach

Instructions: Partners take turns placing letter pattern cards in the word card blanks to make words.

sc____t	sp____k
fl____r	st____t
m____k	t____t
cl____d	c____t
pr____d	ch____t

Compound Word Cards
RallyCoach

Instructions: Cut apart the word cards. Use with the Compound Words Worksheet to make compound words.

Compound Word Card	Compound Word Card	Compound Word Card
bed	snow	cake
sun	house	cow
cup	pop	ball
butter	star	room
brush	fish	rain
corn	tooth	dog
fly	bow	boy
paper	news	hair

Compound Words Worksheet
RallyCoach

Instructions: Partners take turns choosing two words from the compound word cards to form a compound word. One word card is placed in each of the first two columns. The compound word they form is written in the last column.

Word 1	Word 2	Compound Word

Onset Blends and Rimes Word Cards
RallyCoach

Instructions: Partners take turns decoding words. A word card is chosen and a Wikki Stix (formed in a circle) is placed around the onset blend or around the rime (depending on the instructional focus).

Onset Blends and Rimes Word Cards	Onset Blends and Rimes Word Cards
trip	flag
crib	clam
spit	drip
clap	skin

 Balanced Literacy • First Grade • Skidmore & Graber
Kagan Publishing • 1 (800) 933-2667 • www.KaganOnline.com

Onset Blends and Rimes Word Cards
RallyCoach

Instructions: Partners take turns decoding words. A word card is chosen and a Wikki Stix (formed in a circle) is placed around the onset blend or around the rime (depending on the instructional focus).

Onset Blends and Rimes Word Cards	Onset Blends and Rimes Word Cards
slid	grin
Onset Blends and Rimes Word Cards	Onset Blends and Rimes Word Cards
spin	sled
Onset Blends and Rimes Word Cards	Onset Blends and Rimes Word Cards
plum	spot
Onset Blends and Rimes Word Cards	Onset Blends and Rimes Word Cards
plus	slam

Onset Blends and Rimes Word Cards
RallyCoach

Instructions: Partners take turns decoding words. A word card is chosen and a Wikki Stix (formed in a circle) is placed around the onset blend or around the rime (depending on the instructional focus).

Onset Blends and Rimes Word Cards	Onset Blends and Rimes Word Cards
grip	**drum**

Onset Blends and Rimes Word Cards	Onset Blends and Rimes Word Cards
trap	**spun**

Onset Blends and Rimes Word Cards	Onset Blends and Rimes Word Cards
frog	**snap**

Onset Blends and Rimes Word Cards	Onset Blends and Rimes Word Cards
stem	**trim**

Onset Blends and Rimes Word Cards
RallyCoach

Instructions: Partners take turns decoding words. A word card is chosen and a Wikki Stix (formed in a circle) is placed around the onset blend or around the rime (depending on the instructional focus).

Onset Blends and Rimes Word Cards	Onset Blends and Rimes Word Cards
plan	**flit**
Onset Blends and Rimes Word Cards	Onset Blends and Rimes Word Cards
grab	**plug**
Onset Blends and Rimes Word Cards	Onset Blends and Rimes Word Cards
crop	**skip**
Onset Blends and Rimes Word Cards	Onset Blends and Rimes Word Cards
glad	**grid**

Onset Blends and Rimes Word Cards
RallyCoach

Instructions: Partners take turns decoding words. A word card is chosen and a Wikki Stix (formed in a circle) is placed around the onset blend or around the rime (depending on the instructional focus).

Onset Blends and Rimes Word Cards	Onset Blends and Rimes Word Cards
crab	smug
Onset Blends and Rimes Word Cards	Onset Blends and Rimes Word Cards
step	bled
Onset Blends and Rimes Word Cards	Onset Blends and Rimes Word Cards
trot	snip
Onset Blends and Rimes Word Cards	Onset Blends and Rimes Word Cards
flop	brag

Onset Blends and Rimes Word Cards
RallyCoach

Instructions: Partners take turns decoding words. A word card is chosen and a Wikki Stix (formed in a circle) is placed around the onset blend or around the rime (depending on the instructional focus).

Onset Blends and Rimes Word Cards	Onset Blends and Rimes Word Cards
grit	club
slug	slim
plod	snag
slum	bran

Word Endings Word Cards
RallyCoach

Instructions: Partners take turns decoding words. A word card is chosen and a Wikki Stix (formed in a circle) is placed around the word ending to help decode the word.

Word Endings Word Cards **being**	**Word Endings Word Cards** **walked**
Word Endings Word Cards **picking**	**Word Endings Word Cards** **yelled**
Word Endings Word Cards **asked**	**Word Endings Word Cards** **adding**
Word Endings Word Cards **eating**	**Word Endings Word Cards** **filled**

Word Endings Word Cards
RallyCoach

Instructions: Partners take turns decoding words. A word card is chosen and a Wikki Stix (formed in a circle) is placed around the word ending to help decode the word.

Word Endings Word Cards	Word Endings Word Cards
spelled	licked
winked	seeing
clicked	selling
drilled	spilling

Word Endings Word Cards
RallyCoach

Instructions: Partners take turns decoding words. A word card is chosen and a Wikki Stix (formed in a circle) is placed around the word ending to help decode the word.

Word Endings Word Cards	Word Endings Word Cards
chilled	sailed
Word Endings Word Cards	Word Endings Word Cards
calling	dashed
Word Endings Word Cards	Word Endings Word Cards
talked	ticking
Word Endings Word Cards	Word Endings Word Cards
grilled	falling

Sorting Sounds Mat (2 sounds of *ea*)
RallyCoach

Instructions: Copy one mat for each pair. Sort each word into the correct column, according to the sound that *ea* makes in each word. Students may place the word cards in the correct column or write the words.

ea	ea

Word Cards (2 sounds of *ea*)
RallyCoach

Instructions: Copy one set of cards for each pair. Cut apart.

Word Cards	Word Cards
thread	jeans
bean	leaf
sweat	spread
tea	seat
bread	clean
teach	ready
neat	reach
health	wheat
seal	head
leather	bead
beach	read
weather	eat

Sorting Sounds Mat (2 sounds of *ow*)
RallyCoach

Instructions: Copy one mat for each pair. Sort each word into the correct column, according to the sound that *ow* makes in each word. Students may place the word cards in the correct column or write the words.

ow	ow

Word Cards (2 sounds of *ow*)

RallyCoach

Instructions: Copy one set of cards for each pair. Cut apart.

Word Cards		Word Cards	
Word Cards	cow	Word Cards	frown
Word Cards	snow	Word Cards	row
Word Cards	plow	Word Cards	brown
Word Cards	down	Word Cards	throw
Word Cards	glow	Word Cards	bowl
Word Cards	crown	Word Cards	owl
Word Cards	how	Word Cards	slow
Word Cards	own	Word Cards	show
Word Cards	flow	Word Cards	low
Word Cards	town	Word Cards	blow
Word Cards	drown	Word Cards	grow
Word Cards	crow	Word Cards	scowl

Sorting Sounds Mat (2 sounds of *oo*)
RallyCoach

Instructions: Copy one mat for each pair. Sort each word into the correct column, according to the sound that *oo* makes in each word. Students may place the word cards in the correct column or write the words.

oo	oo

Word Cards (2 sounds of *oo*)
RallyCoach

Instructions: Copy one set of cards for each pair. Cut apart.

Word Cards	Word Cards
book	roof
room	food
school	goose
cool	look
stool	boot
foot	tool
zoom	wood
cook	broom
noon	good
hood	moon
stood	zoo
soon	wool

Word Study Showdown

Teams play Showdown to practice word parts, rhyming words, letter patterns, and word patterns.

STRUCTURE

Showdown

Note:
The teacher is the Showdown Captain, rather than rotating the responsibility among the team. This activity can also be done with partners.

Activity Steps

1. Each team receives a Team Set of cards. If the teacher is the Showdown Captain, make 1 overhead transparency in place of Team Cards. Every student receives a Student Set of cards.

2. The Team Set is placed facedown in the middle of the team. Or, if the teacher is the Showdown Captain, one card is placed on the overhead at a time. Students hold their Student set in their hands.

3. The teacher is the Showdown Captain or selects one student to be the Showdown Captain for the first round.

4. The Showdown Captain (teacher) selects the top card from the middle and reads it aloud.

5. Working alone, students individually identify an answer from their card set.

6. When finished, teammates signal they are ready.

7. The Showdown Captain (teacher) calls, "Showdown!"

8. Teammates show their answers at the same time.

9. Showdown Captain (teacher) leads checking.

10. If correct, the team celebrates. If not, the teammates coach, then celebrate.

11. The person to the left of the Showdown Captain becomes the Showdown Captain for the next round. Or, the teacher continues as Showdown Captain.

Activities

Word Study Showdown (continued)

Teams play Showdown to practice word parts, rhyming words, letter patterns, and word patterns.

Blacklines

Word Parts Word Cards
Showdown (Card Set 1)

Instructions: Copy one set of cards for each pair or make a transparency if teacher is the Showdown Captain.

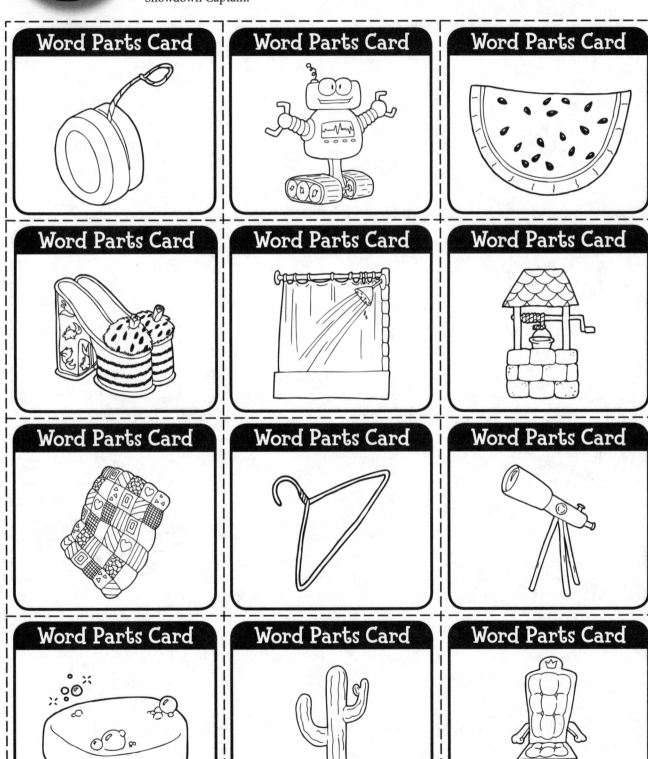

Word Parts Card	Word Parts Card	Word Parts Card
Word Parts Card	Word Parts Card	Word Parts Card
Word Parts Card	Word Parts Card	Word Parts Card
Word Parts Card	Word Parts Card	Word Parts Card

Word Parts Word Cards
Showdown (Card Set 1)

Instructions: Copy one set of cards for each pair or make a transparency if teacher is the Showdown Captain.

Word Parts Card	Word Parts Card	Word Parts Card
	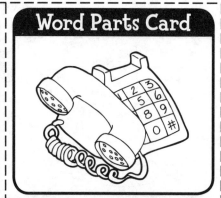	

Word Parts Card	Word Parts Card	Word Parts Card

Word Parts Card	Word Parts Card	Word Parts Card

Word Parts Card	Word Parts Card	Word Parts Card

Word Parts Word Cards

Showdown (Card Set 1)

Instructions: Copy one set of cards for each pair or make a transparency if teacher is the Showdown Captain.

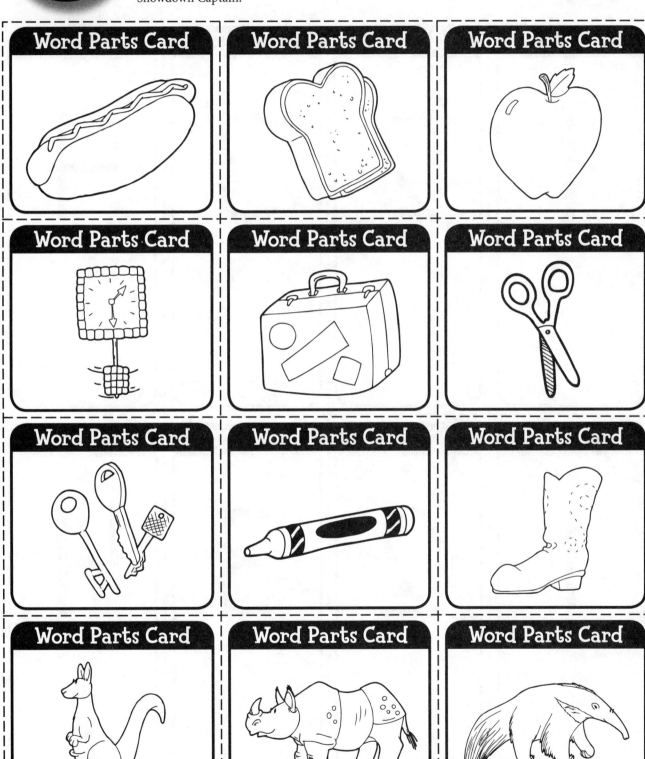

Word Parts Card	Word Parts Card	Word Parts Card
Word Parts Card	Word Parts Card	Word Parts Card
Word Parts Card	Word Parts Card	Word Parts Card
Word Parts Card	Word Parts Card	Word Parts Card

Number of Word Parts Cards
Showdown (Card Set 2 for students)

Instructions: This page has cards for two students. Copy, cut apart, and give each student one set of numbered cards 1–4.

Number of Word Parts Card	Number of Word Parts Card	Number of Word Parts Card	Number of Word Parts Card
1	2	3	4

Number of Word Parts Card	Number of Word Parts Card	Number of Word Parts Card	Number of Word Parts Card
1	2	3	4

Rhyming Words
Showdown (Card Set 1)

Instructions: Copy one set of cards for each team or make a transparency if teacher is the Showdown Captain.

Rhyming Words Card

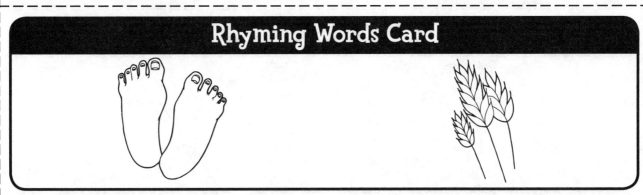

Rhyming Words Card

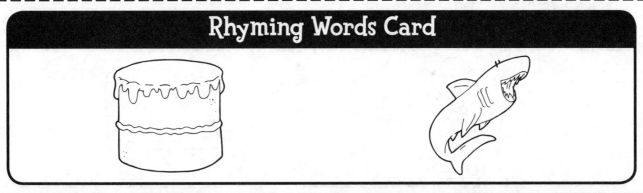

Rhyming Words Card

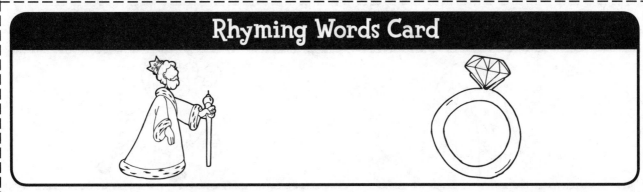

Rhyming Words Card

Rhyming Words
Showdown (Card Set 1)

Instructions: Copy one set of cards for each team or make a transparency if teacher is the Showdown Captain.

Rhyming Words Card

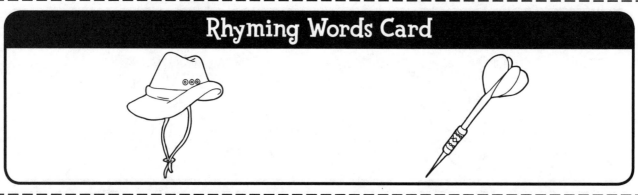

Rhyming Words Card

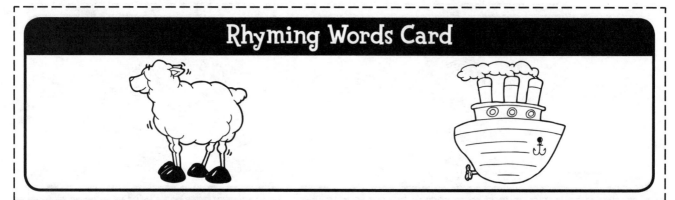

Rhyming Words Card

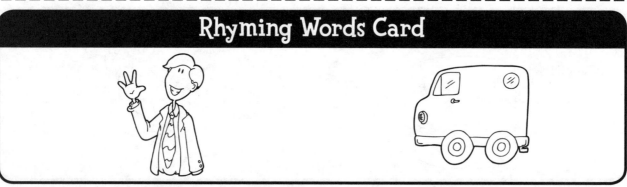

Rhyming Words Card

Rhyming Words
Showdown (Card Set 1)

Instructions: Copy one set of cards for each team or make a transparency if teacher is the Showdown Captain.

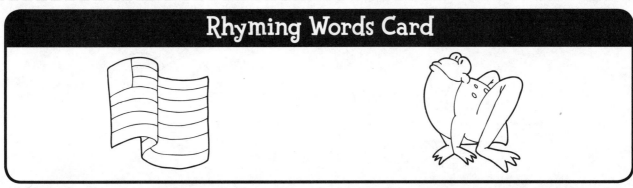

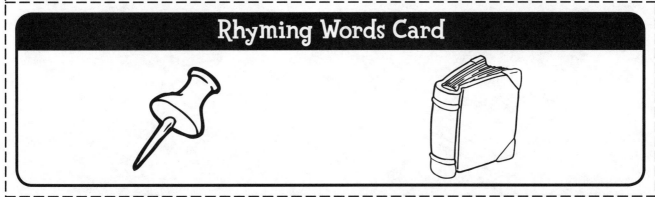

Rhyming Words
Showdown (Card Set 1)

Instructions: Copy one set of cards for each team or make a transparency if teacher is the Showdown Captain.

Rhyming Words Card

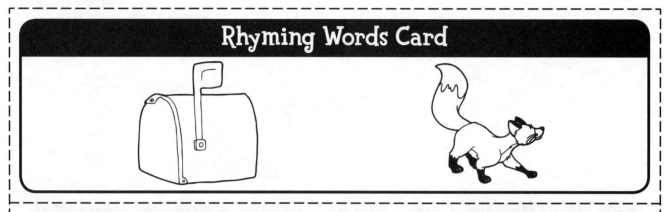

Rhyming Words Card

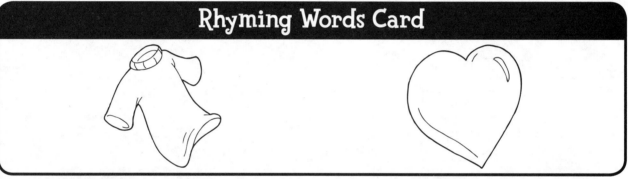

Rhyming Words Card

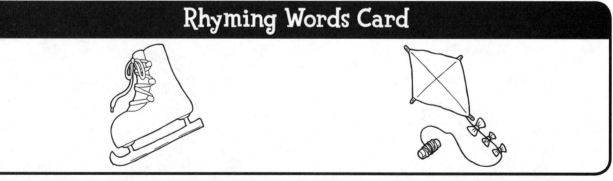

Rhyming Words Card

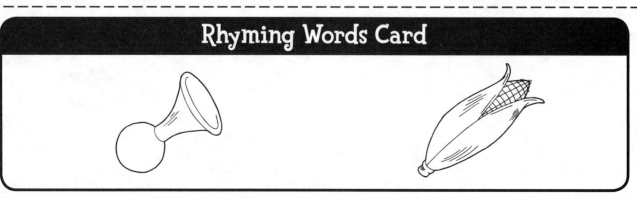

Rhyming Yes/No Cards

Showdown (Student Set)

Note: This page has cards for four students (one team). Copy, cut apart, and give each student one set of Yes/No cards.

Rhyming Yes/No Cards Student Set	Rhyming Yes/No Cards Student Set	Rhyming Yes/No Cards Student Set	Rhyming Yes/No Cards Student Set
yes	no	yes	no

Rhyming Yes/No Cards Student Set	Rhyming Yes/No Cards Student Set	Rhyming Yes/No Cards Student Set	Rhyming Yes/No Cards Student Set
yes	no	yes	no

Teacher Word List (ch, sh, th, wh)
Showdown

Instructions: The teacher reads these words orally, one at a time, as individual students in teams choose the Showdown Card that shows whether a ch, sh, th, or wh sound is heard in the word. Follow the Showdown structure directions.

1. <u>wh</u>ale	17. <u>ch</u>icken
2. wi<u>th</u>	18. <u>wh</u>istle
3. <u>sh</u>ake	19. tee<u>th</u>
4. wat<u>ch</u>	20. ca<u>sh</u>
5. <u>th</u>under	21. fi<u>sh</u>ing
6. <u>th</u>ink	22. <u>wh</u>eel
7. cra<u>sh</u>	23. per<u>ch</u>
8. <u>wh</u>isper	24. da<u>sh</u>
9. <u>th</u>irsty	25. pin<u>ch</u>
10. sma<u>sh</u>	26. <u>ch</u>op
11. <u>wh</u>eat	27. ga<u>sh</u>
12. <u>th</u>irteen	28. <u>th</u>irty
13. tra<u>sh</u>	29. wi<u>sh</u>ing
14. sear<u>ch</u>	30. <u>ch</u>erry
15. <u>wh</u>ite	31. sun<u>sh</u>ine
16. ra<u>sh</u>	

Balanced Literacy • First Grade • Skidmore & Graber
Kagan Publishing • 1 (800) 933-2667 • www.KaganOnline.com

Letter Patterns—Listening Activity Cards
(ch, sh, th, wh)
Showdown

Instructions: This page has cards for two students. Copy, cut apart, and give each student one set of cards.

Letter Patterns—Listening Activity Cards	Letter Patterns—Listening Activity Cards	Letter Patterns—Listening Activity Cards	Letter Patterns—Listening Activity Cards
ch	sh	th	wh
Letter Patterns—Listening Activity Cards	Letter Patterns—Listening Activity Cards	Letter Patterns—Listening Activity Cards	Letter Patterns—Listening Activity Cards
ch	sh	th	wh

Teacher Word List (_all, _ell, _ill)
Showdown

Instructions: The teacher reads these words orally, one at a time, as individual students in teams choose the Showdown Card that shows the rime heard in the word. Follow the Showdown structure directions.

1. b<u>ill</u>	16. h<u>all</u>
2. w<u>ell</u>	17. ch<u>ill</u>
3. gr<u>ill</u>	18. s<u>ell</u>
4. f<u>all</u>	19. w<u>ill</u>
5. tw<u>ill</u>	20. st<u>ill</u>
6. b<u>ell</u>	21. t<u>ell</u>
7. m<u>all</u>	22. t<u>all</u>
8. h<u>ill</u>	23. p<u>ill</u>
9. sw<u>ell</u>	24. sp<u>ell</u>
10. thr<u>ill</u>	25. sk<u>ill</u>
11. w<u>all</u>	26. f<u>ill</u>
12. sh<u>ell</u>	27. d<u>ill</u>
13. b<u>all</u>	28. sp<u>ill</u>
14. sh<u>all</u>	29. c<u>all</u>
15. tr<u>ill</u>	30. gr<u>ill</u>

Word Patterns—Listening Activity Cards
(_all, _ell, _ill)
Showdown

Instructions: This page has cards for two students. Copy, cut apart, and give each student one set of cards.

Word Patterns—
Listening Activity Cards

_all

Word Patterns—
Listening Activity Cards

_ell

Word Patterns—
Listening Activity Cards

_ill

Word Patterns—
Listening Activity Cards

_all

Word Patterns—
Listening Activity Cards

_ell

Word Patterns—
Listening Activity Cards

_ill

Teacher Word List (_ang, _ing, _ong)
Showdown

Instructions: The teacher reads these words orally, one at a time, as individual students in teams choose the Showdown Card that shows the rime heard in the word. Follow the Showdown structure directions.

1. song	10. rang
2. king	11. dong
3. sang	12. wing
4. long	13. wrong
5. ring	14. bang
6. fang	15. string
7. strong	16. hang
8. thing	17. spring
9. bring	18. swing

Word Patterns–Listening Activity Cards
(_ang, _ing, _ong)
Showdown

Instructions: This page has cards for two students. Copy, cut apart, and give each student one set of cards.

Word Patterns–
Listening Activity Cards

_ang

Word Patterns–
Listening Activity Cards

_ing

Word Patterns–
Listening Activity Cards

_ong

Word Patterns–
Listening Activity Cards

_ang

Word Patterns–
Listening Activity Cards

_ing

Word Patterns–
Listening Activity Cards

_ong

Teacher Word List (_ank, _ink, _unk)
Showdown

Instructions: The teacher reads these words orally, one at a time, as individual students in teams choose the Showdown Card that which shows the rime heard in the word. Follow the Showdown structure directions.

1. b<u>ank</u>	15. shr<u>ink</u>
2. th<u>ink</u>	16. s<u>ink</u>
3. p<u>ink</u>	17. bl<u>ank</u>
4. s<u>unk</u>	18. shr<u>unk</u>
5. dr<u>ank</u>	19. tr<u>unk</u>
6. kerpl<u>unk</u>	20. bl<u>ink</u>
7. dr<u>ink</u>	21. j<u>unk</u>
8. th<u>ank</u>	22. cl<u>ink</u>
9. dr<u>unk</u>	23. m<u>ink</u>
10. w<u>ink</u>	24. pr<u>ank</u>
11. r<u>ink</u>	25. ch<u>unk</u>
12. s<u>ank</u>	26. l<u>ink</u>
13. d<u>unk</u>	27. h<u>unk</u>
14. t<u>ank</u>	28. y<u>ank</u>

Balanced Literacy • First Grade • Skidmore & Graber
Kagan Publishing • 1 (800) 933-2667 • www.KaganOnline.com

Word Patterns—Listening Activity Cards
(_ank, _ink, _unk)
Showdown

Instructions: This page has cards for two students. Copy, cut apart, and give each student one set of cards.

Word Patterns— Listening Activity Cards	Word Patterns— Listening Activity Cards	Word Patterns— Listening Activity Cards
_ank	_ink	_unk
_ank	_ink	_unk

Activities

Simultaneous RallyTable

In pairs, students alternate generating written responses or solving problems.

Activity Steps

1. Teacher assigns the word rime strips or beginning letter strips to be used from the following pages.

2. In pairs, students each have a word strip. Each writes one word at the same time and then trade at the same time.

3. Continue writing and trading word strips until time is called.

Centerpiece

Students brainstorm words to add to the list, always trading their paper with the centerpiece.

STRUCTURE

Simultaneous RallyTable or CenterPiece

Activity Steps

1. Teacher assigns the word rime strips or beginning letter strips to be used from the following pages.

2. Students generate words to include on the word strips. They say the word, write it, and trade their paper with the one in the center.

3. Students continue brainstorming items, each time trading their paper with the centerpiece.

Blacklines

Onsets and Rimes Word Strips
Simultaneous RallyTable or Centerpiece

Instructions: <u>Simultaneous RallyTable</u>: For each pair of students, copy and cut apart two different Rime Strips for them to exchange back and forth as they write words that rhyme by adding a single consonant or blend onset. <u>Centerpiece</u>: Copy and cut apart a different rime strip for each student in the team or pair, plus one extra, so during the activity there is always one in the center to trade with.

Onsets and Rimes Word Strip | _ip

Onsets and Rimes Word Strip | _it

Onsets and Rimes Word Strip | _ot

Onsets and Rimes Word Strip | _ug

Onsets and Rimes Word Strips
Simultaneous RallyTable or Centerpiece

Instructions: <u>Simultaneous RallyTable</u>: For each pair of students, copy and cut apart two different Rime Strips for them to exchange back and forth as they write words that rhyme by adding a single consonant or blend onset. <u>Centerpiece</u>: Copy and cut apart a different rime strip for each student in the team or pair, plus one extra, so during the activity there is always one in the center to trade with.

Onsets and Rimes Word Strip

_ock

Onsets and Rimes Word Strip

_ack

Onsets and Rimes Word Strip

_ill

Onsets and Rimes Word Strip

_ell

Onsets and Rimes Word Strips
Simultaneous RallyTable or Centerpiece

Instructions: <u>Simultaneous RallyTable:</u> For each pair of students, copy and cut apart two different Rime Strips for them to exchange back and forth as they write words that rhyme by adding a single consonant or blend onset. <u>Centerpiece:</u> Copy and cut apart a different rime strip for each student in the team or pair, plus one extra, so during the activity there is always one in the center to trade with.

Onsets and Rimes Word Strip **_unk**

Onsets and Rimes Word Strip **_ick**

Onsets and Rimes Word Strip **_ash**

Onsets and Rimes Word Strip **_ump**

Onsets and Rimes Word Strips
Simultaneous RallyTable or Centerpiece

Instructions: <u>Simultaneous RallyTable</u>: For each pair of students, copy and cut apart two different Rime Strips for them to exchange back and forth as they write words that rhyme by adding a single consonant or blend onset. <u>Centerpiece</u>: Copy and cut apart a different rime strip for each student in the team or pair, plus one extra, so during the activity there is always one in the center to trade with.

Onsets and Rimes Word Strip

_ide

Onsets and Rimes Word Strip

_ay

Onsets and Rimes Word Strip

_ame

Onsets and Rimes Word Strip

_ail

Onsets and Rimes Form
Simultaneous RallyTable or Centerpiece

Instructions: Fill in top space on strips with desired rimes. <u>Simultaneous RallyTable</u>: For each pair of students, copy and cut apart two different Rime Strips for them to exchange back and forth as they write words that rhyme by adding a single consonant or blend onset. <u>Centerpiece</u>: Copy and cut apart a different rime strip for each student in the team or pair, plus one extra, so during the activity there is always one in the center to trade with.

Onsets and Rimes Form

Onsets and Rimes Form

Onsets and Rimes Form

Onsets and Rimes Form

Onsets and Rimes A-Z Reference Strips
Simultaneous RallyTable or Centerpiece

Instructions: Cut apart strips for each student or pair of students to use as a reference when choosing onsets to add to the rime strip to make words.

a	b	c	d	e	f	g	h	i	j	k	l	m	n	o	p	q	r	s	t	u	v	w	x	y	z
A	B	C	D	E	F	G	H	I	J	K	L	M	N	O	P	Q	R	S	T	U	V	W	X	Y	Z

a	b	c	d	e	f	g	h	i	j	k	l	m	n	o	p	q	r	s	t	u	v	w	x	y	z
A	B	C	D	E	F	G	H	I	J	K	L	M	N	O	P	Q	R	S	T	U	V	W	X	Y	Z

a	b	c	d	e	f	g	h	i	j	k	l	m	n	o	p	q	r	s	t	u	v	w	x	y	z
A	B	C	D	E	F	G	H	I	J	K	L	M	N	O	P	Q	R	S	T	U	V	W	X	Y	Z

a	b	c	d	e	f	g	h	i	j	k	l	m	n	o	p	q	r	s	t	u	v	w	x	y	z
A	B	C	D	E	F	G	H	I	J	K	L	M	N	O	P	Q	R	S	T	U	V	W	X	Y	Z

Beginning Letter Strips
Simultaneous RallyTable or Centerpiece

Instructions: <u>Simultaneous RallyTable</u>: For each pair of students, copy and cut apart different Beginning Letter Strips for them to exchange back and forth as they add words that begin with the letter at the top. <u>Centerpiece</u>: Copy and cut apart a different Beginning Letter Strip for each student in the team or pair, plus one extra, so during the activity there is always one in the center to trade with.

Onsets and Rimes Beginning Letters

p

Onsets and Rimes Beginning Letters

m

Onsets and Rimes Beginning Letters

b

Onsets and Rimes Beginning Letters

s

Beginning Letter Strips
Simultaneous RallyTable or Centerpiece

Instructions: <u>Simultaneous RallyTable:</u> For each pair of students, copy and cut apart different Beginning Letter Strips for them to exchange back and forth as they add words that begin with the letter at the top. <u>Centerpiece:</u> Copy and cut apart a different Beginning Letter Strip for each student in the team or pair, plus one extra, so during the activity there is always one in the center to trade with.

Onsets and Rimes Beginning Letters

t

Onsets and Rimes Beginning Letters

n

Onsets and Rimes Beginning Letters

p

Onsets and Rimes Beginning Letters

r

Balanced Literacy • First Grade • Skidmore & Graber
Kagan Publishing • 1 (800) 933-2667 • www.KaganOnline.com

Beginning Letters Form
Simultaneous RallyTable or Centerpiece

Instructions: Fill in top space on strips with desired beginning letters. <u>Simultaneous RallyTable</u>: For each pair of students, copy and cut apart different Beginning Letter Strips for them to exchange back and forth as they add words that begin with the letter at the top. <u>Centerpiece</u>: Copy and cut apart a different Beginning Letter Strip for each student in the team or pair, plus one extra, so during the activity there is always one in the center to trade with.

Onsets and Rimes Beginning Letters

Onsets and Rimes Beginning Letters

Onsets and Rimes Beginning Letters

Onsets and Rimes Beginning Letters

Activity

Word Wall Spelling

After spelling the word themselves, teammates put their "heads together" to ensure all members can correctly spell the word wall word. The teacher then calls a number and all students with that number share their team's spelling.

Activity Steps

1. Students number off in small groups.

2. Teacher reads a selected word from the Word List.

3. Students privately write the word on a markerboard or on a piece of paper.

4. Teacher says, "Heads Together!" and students lift up from their chairs to put their heads together, show their answers, and discuss until they reach consensus on the word spelling.

5. Everyone clears their boards and sits down when they agree.

6. The teacher calls out a number. All students with that number write the agreed-upon spelling of the word on their markerboards.

7. All students with their number selected hold up their boards simultaneously. The teacher writes each group's spelling on the overhead.

8. The teacher leads the class in a discussion of each spelling by asking questions such as "Which way looks right?" "How do you know?" or "What was the tricky part or familiar part?"

9. Teammates celebrate or correct spelling on boards.

10. The process is repeated for each new word.

Note: "Words With/Without Silent e Word List" provides extra word choices.

STRUCTURE

Numbered Heads Together

Note:
The Word Wall Cards on the following pages are not used for this activity. They are provided for your convenience to post on your Word Wall. However, before you begin this activity, make sure you take down Word Wall words students will spell.

Blacklines

First Grade Word List

Numbered Heads Together

Instructions: Words to be used with Word Wall Spelling.

a	go	on	what
all	had	one	with
am	have	or	you
and	he	see	your
are	his	so	
as	I	that	
at	in	the	
be	is	they	
but	it	this	
by	like	to	
can	me	up	
do	my	was	
for	not	we	
from	of	were	

First Grade
Word Wall Cards
Numbered Heads Together

Instructions: Use the cards provided to create a Word Wall.

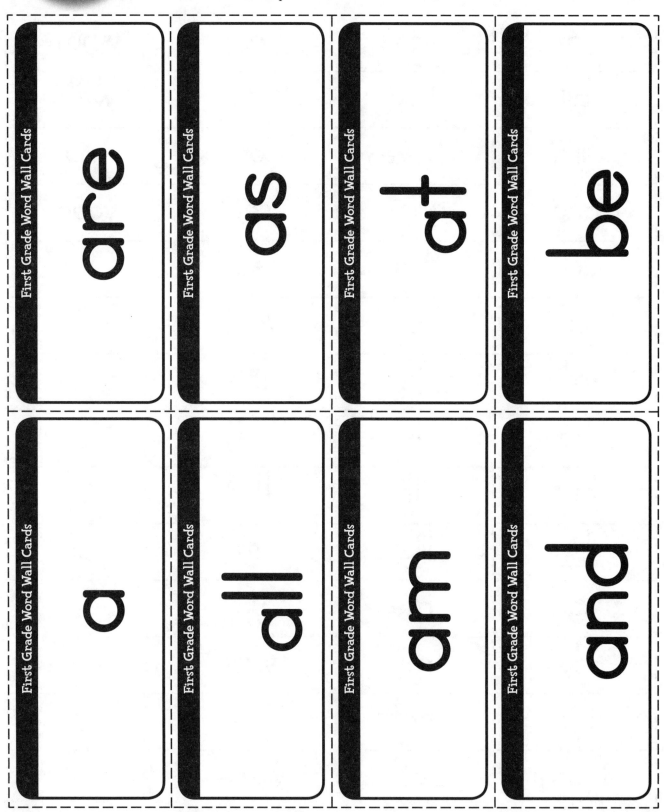

First Grade Word Wall Cards	First Grade Word Wall Cards	First Grade Word Wall Cards	First Grade Word Wall Cards
are	as	at	be
a	all	am	and

First Grade
Word Wall Cards
Numbered Heads Together

Instructions: Use the cards provided to create a Word Wall.

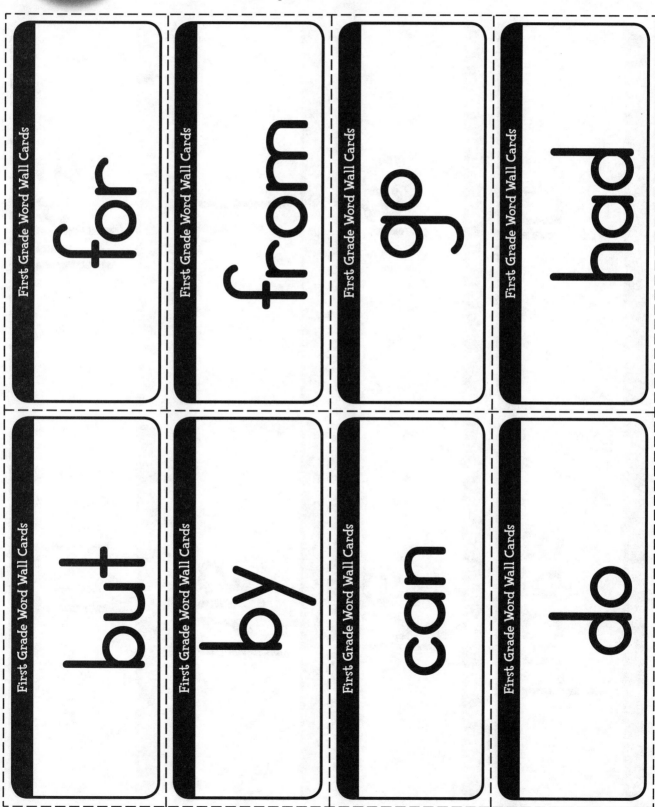

First Grade Word Wall Cards

for

First Grade Word Wall Cards

from

First Grade Word Wall Cards

go

First Grade Word Wall Cards

had

First Grade Word Wall Cards

but

First Grade Word Wall Cards

by

First Grade Word Wall Cards

can

First Grade Word Wall Cards

do

First Grade
Word Wall Cards

Numbered Heads Together

Instructions: Use the cards provided to create a Word Wall.

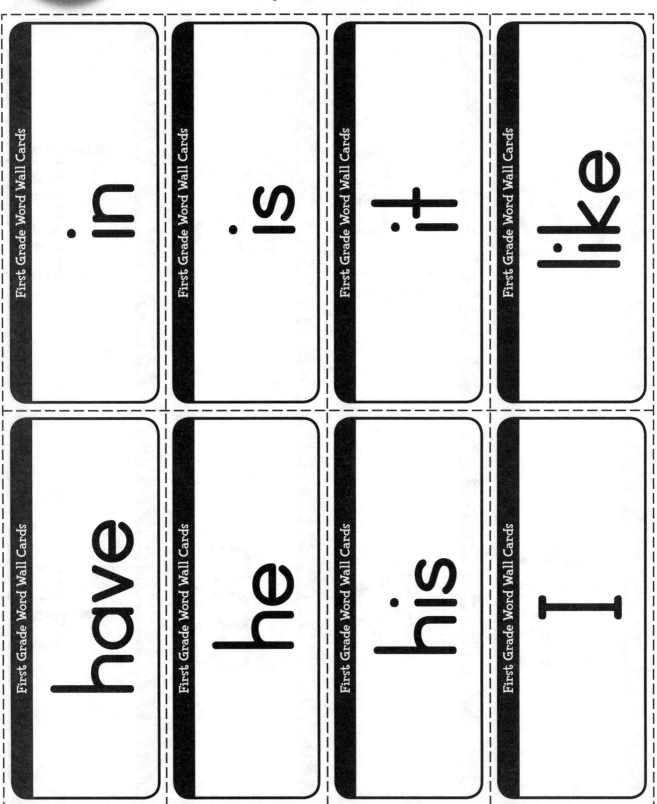

First Grade Word Wall Cards	First Grade Word Wall Cards	First Grade Word Wall Cards	First Grade Word Wall Cards
in	is	it	like
have	he	his	I

Balanced Literacy • First Grade • Skidmore & Graber
Kagan Publishing • 1 (800) 933-2667 • www.KaganOnline.com

First Grade
Word Wall Cards
Numbered Heads Together

Instructions: Use the cards provided to create a Word Wall.

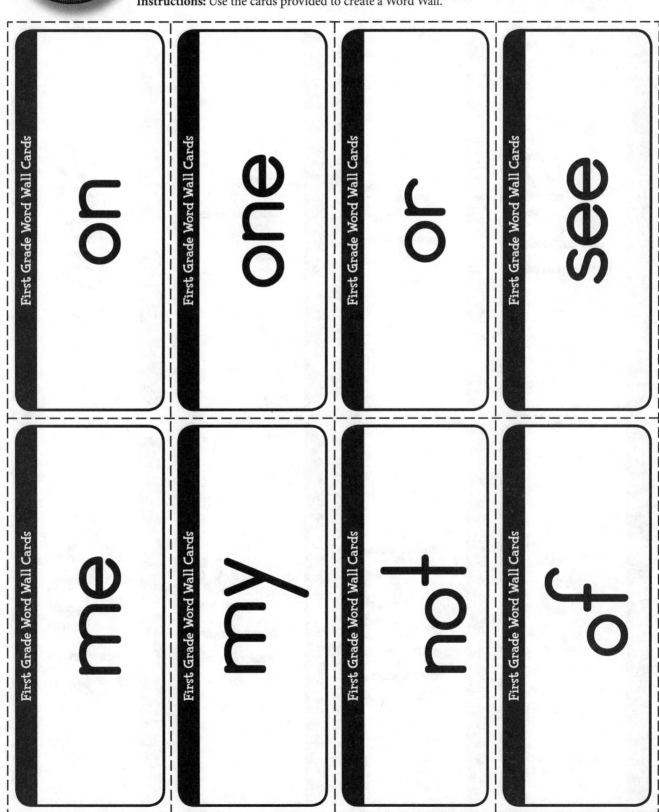

First Grade Word Wall Cards

on

First Grade Word Wall Cards

one

First Grade Word Wall Cards

or

First Grade Word Wall Cards

see

First Grade Word Wall Cards

me

First Grade Word Wall Cards

my

First Grade Word Wall Cards

not

First Grade Word Wall Cards

of

First Grade
Word Wall Cards

Numbered Heads Together

Instructions: Use the cards provided to create a Word Wall.

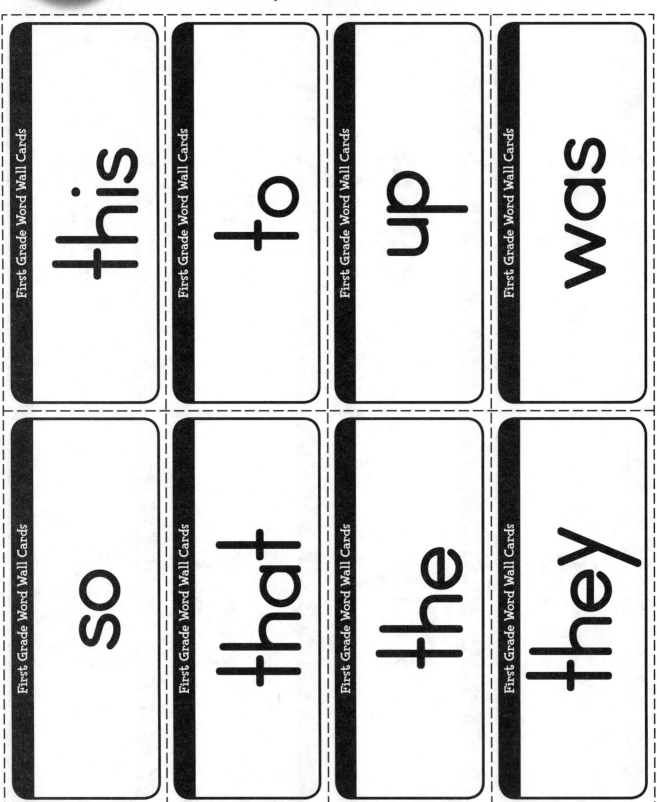

First Grade Word Wall Cards — **this**

First Grade Word Wall Cards — **to**

First Grade Word Wall Cards — **up**

First Grade Word Wall Cards — **was**

First Grade Word Wall Cards — **so**

First Grade Word Wall Cards — **that**

First Grade Word Wall Cards — **the**

First Grade Word Wall Cards — **they**

Balanced Literacy • First Grade • Skidmore & Graber
Kagan Publishing • 1 (800) 933-2667 • www.KaganOnline.com

First Grade
Word Wall Cards

Numbered Heads Together

Instructions: Use the cards provided to create a Word Wall.

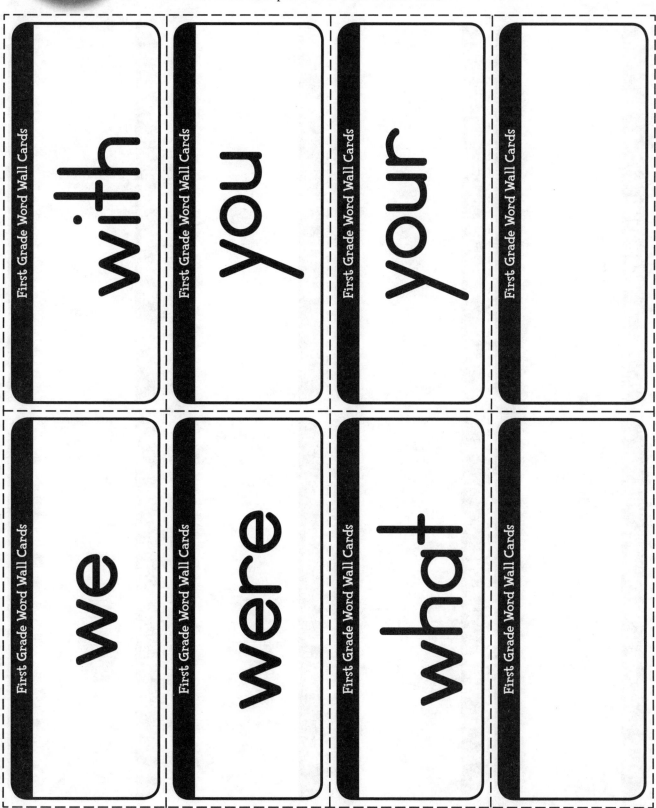

First Grade Word Wall Cards

with

First Grade Word Wall Cards

you

First Grade Word Wall Cards

your

First Grade Word Wall Cards

First Grade Word Wall Cards

we

First Grade Word Wall Cards

were

First Grade Word Wall Cards

what

First Grade Word Wall Cards

First Grade
Blank Word Wall Cards
Numbered Heads Together

Instructions: Add additional words to these cards for the Word Wall.

First Grade Word Wall Cards

First Grade Word Wall Cards

First Grade Word Wall Cards

First Grade Word Wall Cards

First Grade Word Wall Cards

First Grade Word Wall Cards

First Grade Word Wall Cards

First Grade Word Wall Cards

Balanced Literacy • First Grade • Skidmore & Graber
Kagan Publishing • 1 (800) 933-2667 • www.KaganOnline.com

Words With/Without Silent e

Numbered Heads Together

Instructions: Teacher list of words to be used with Word Wall Spelling.

not	note	man	mane
kit	kite	van	vane
pin	pine	fin	fine
dim	dime	tub	tube
hop	hope	rob	robe
at	ate	hat	hate
cut	cute	can	cane
rip	ripe	grim	grime
tap	tape	rat	rate
bit	bite	fad	fade
pal	pale	cap	cape
hid	hide	pan	pane
plan	plane		
spin	spine		
slid	slide		
hug	huge		

Word Cards
With/Without Silent e
Numbered Heads Together

Instructions: Use the cards provided to create a Word Wall.

Word Cards With/Without Silent e **note**	Word Cards With/Without Silent e **kite**	Word Cards With/Without Silent e **pine**	Word Cards With/Without Silent e **dime**
Word Cards With/Without Silent e **not**	Word Cards With/Without Silent e **kit**	Word Cards With/Without Silent e **pin**	Word Cards With/Without Silent e **dim**

Balanced Literacy • First Grade • Skidmore & Graber
Kagan Publishing • 1 (800) 933-2667 • www.KaganOnline.com

Word Cards
With/Without Silent e
Numbered Heads Together

Instructions: Use the cards provided to create a Word Wall.

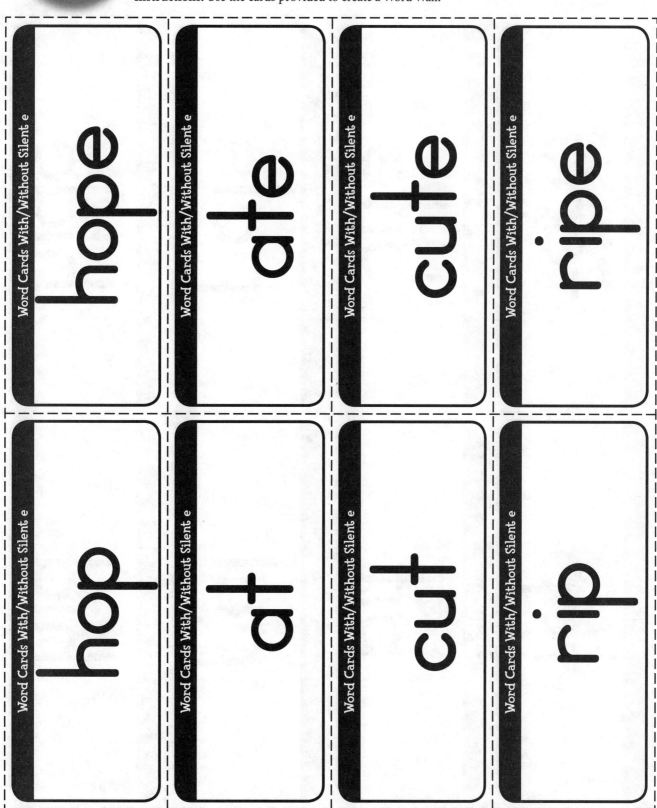

Word Cards With/Without Silent e — hope

Word Cards With/Without Silent e — ate

Word Cards With/Without Silent e — cute

Word Cards With/Without Silent e — ripe

Word Cards With/Without Silent e — hop

Word Cards With/Without Silent e — at

Word Cards With/Without Silent e — cut

Word Cards With/Without Silent e — rip

Word Cards
With/Without Silent e
Numbered Heads Together

Instructions: Use the cards provided to create a Word Wall.

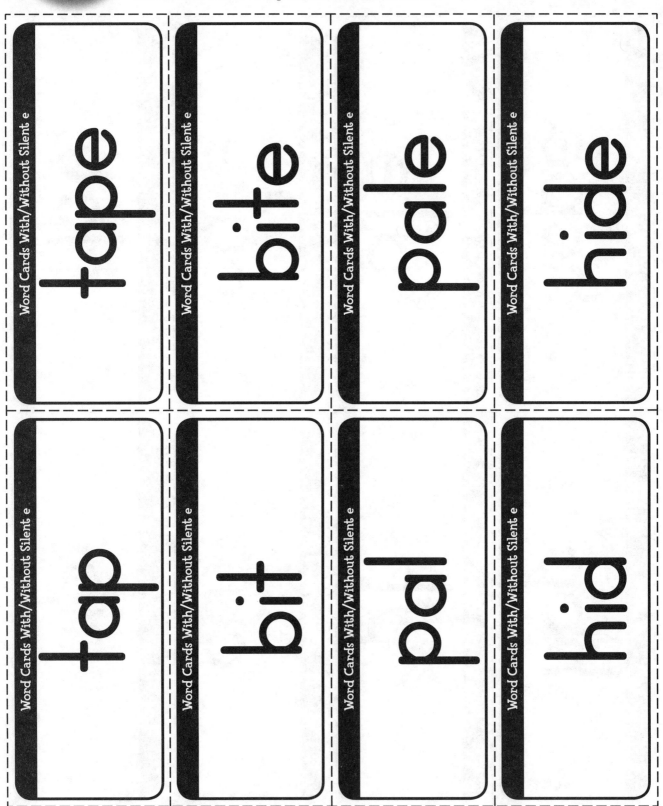

Word Cards With/Without Silent e **tape**	Word Cards With/Without Silent e **bite**	Word Cards With/Without Silent e **pae**	Word Cards With/Without Silent e **hide**
Word Cards With/Without Silent e **tap**	Word Cards With/Without Silent e **bit**	Word Cards With/Without Silent e **pal**	Word Cards With/Without Silent e **hid**

Word Cards
With/Without Silent e
Numbered Heads Together

Instructions: Use the cards provided to create a Word Wall.

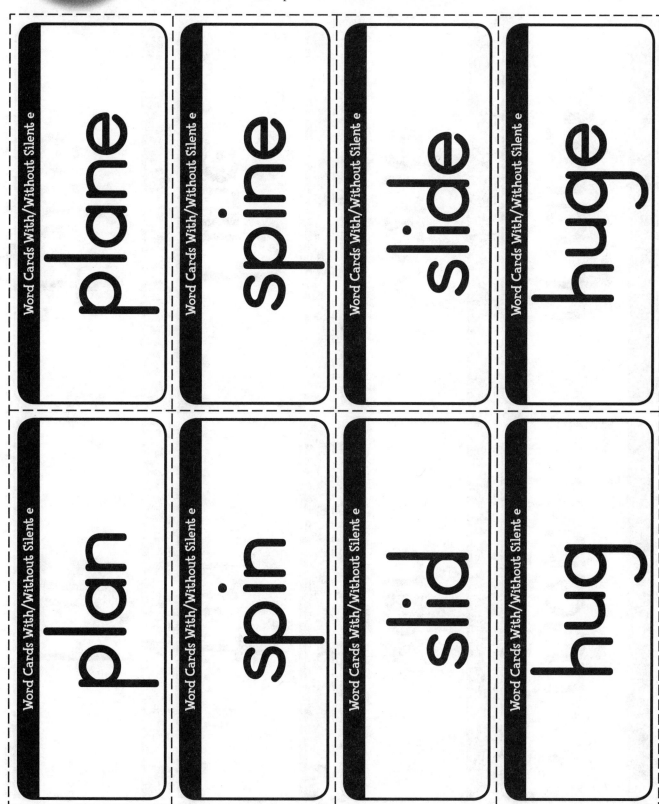

Word Cards With/Without Silent e — plane

Word Cards With/Without Silent e — spine

Word Cards With/Without Silent e — slide

Word Cards With/Without Silent e — huge

Word Cards With/Without Silent e — plan

Word Cards With/Without Silent e — spin

Word Cards With/Without Silent e — slid

Word Cards With/Without Silent e — hug

Word Cards
With/Without Silent e
Numbered Heads Together

Instructions: Use the cards provided to create a Word Wall.

Word Cards With/Without Silent e	Word Cards With/Without Silent e	Word Cards With/Without Silent e	Word Cards With/Without Silent e
mane	vane	fine	tube
man	van	fin	tub

Word Cards
With/Without Silent e

Numbered Heads Together

Instructions: Use the cards provided to create a Word Wall.

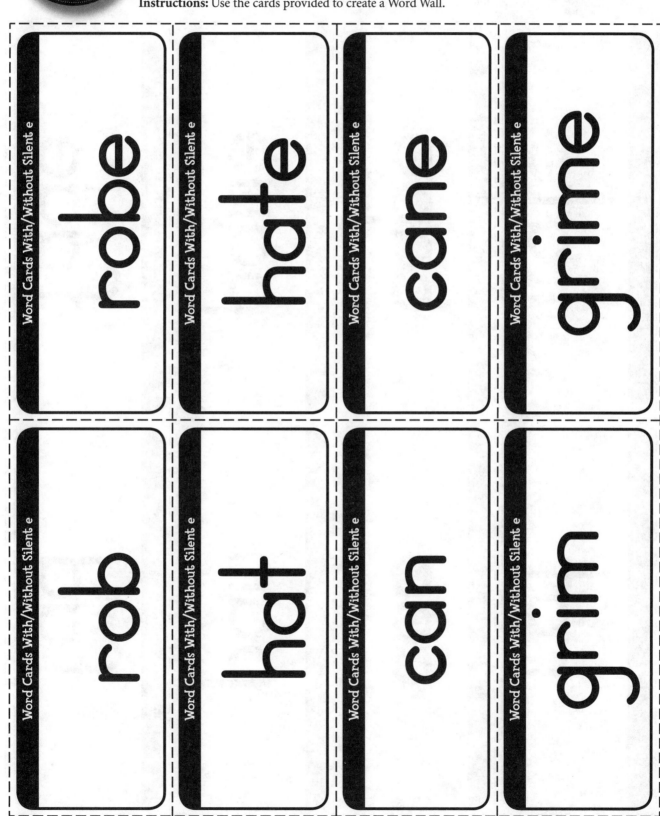

Word Cards With/Without Silent e

robe

Word Cards With/Without Silent e

hate

Word Cards With/Without Silent e

cane

Word Cards With/Without Silent e

grime

Word Cards With/Without Silent e

rob

Word Cards With/Without Silent e

hat

Word Cards With/Without Silent e

can

Word Cards With/Without Silent e

grim

Word Cards
With/Without Silent e
Numbered Heads Together

Instructions: Use the cards provided to create a Word Wall.

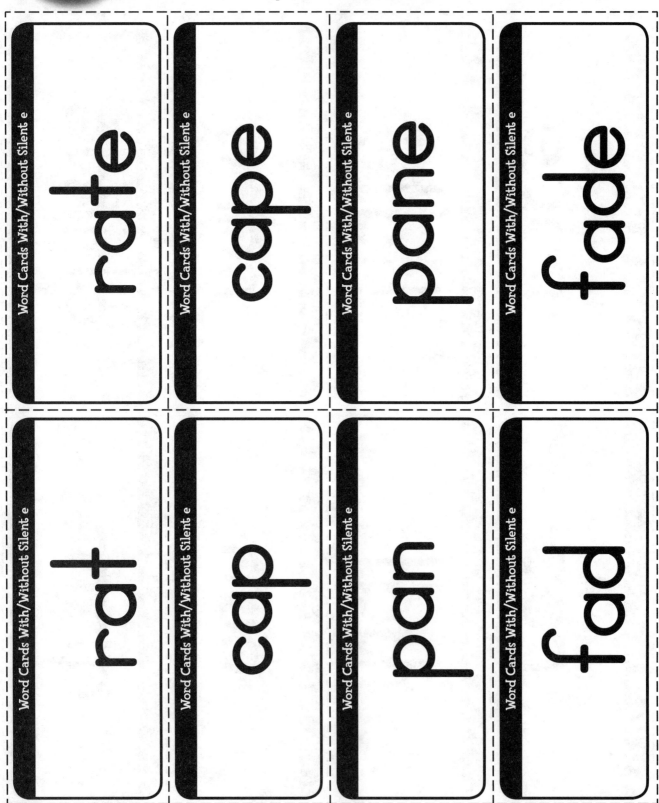

Word Cards With/Without Silent e	Word Cards With/Without Silent e	Word Cards With/Without Silent e	Word Cards With/Without Silent e
rate	**cape**	**pane**	**fade**
rat	**cap**	**pan**	**fad**

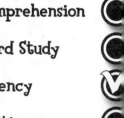

Balanced Literacy

Comprehension

Word Study

Fluency

Writing

Fluency

Fluency Overview

Fluency is a part of an effective reading program. When a reader is fluent, energies are automatically channeled into comprehending the text instead of decoding words.

Reading fluency includes the following components:
- expression (stress, pitch, volume, clarity)
- phrasing (pauses, word groups)
- rate (just the right speed)
- accuracy (correct words and pronunciation)

The fluency resources and materials at the beginning of this section are designed to be used in the suggested order to scaffold the learner and ensure understanding (*aloud* and *shared*). The remainder of the activities in this section are designed to provide fluency practice (*guided* and *independent*).

Table of Decoding and Fluency Resources

Table of Fluency Activities

Page(s)	Activities	Blacklines	Balanced Literacy				
			Aloud	Shared	Guided	Independent	Literature Circles
270	**RallyCoach Activity—Fluency Scoring**						
271	Expression	• Rubric and Graph	●	●	●	●	●
272	Phrasing	• Rubric and Graph	●	●	●	●	●
273	Accuracy	• Rubric and Graph	●	●	●	●	●
274	Rate	• Rubric and Graph	●	●	●	●	●
275	Fluency	• Continuum Worksheet	●	●	●	●	●
276	**Poems for Two Voices Activity—Fluency Poems**						
277	Hiding from the Rain	• Copy of Poem		●	●		
278	Rhyme Time	• Copy of Poem		●	●		
280	Blank Form	• Blank Worksheet		●	●		
281	**Quiz-Quiz-Trade Activity—Fluency**						
282	Sight Word Practice	• Cards		●		●	
287	Fluency Word Phrases	• Cards		●	●	●	
297	Fluency Sentences	• Cards		●	●	●	
305	**Showdown Activity—Punctuation Showdown**						
306	Ending Punctuation (. ?)	• Sentence Strips • Punctuation Cards		●	●	●	
308	Ending Punctuation (. ? !)	• Sentence Strips • Punctuation Cards		●	●	●	

Balanced Literacy • First Grade • Skidmore & Graber
Kagan Publishing • 1 (800) 933-2667 • www.KaganOnline.com

Decoding and Fluency Resources

Resources/Materials Descriptions

Decoding Strategy Bookmarks (p. 262)

The decoding strategy bookmark is a visual prompting tool for students to use as they learn and practice reading strategies.

Decoding Flashcards (pp. 263–264)

(Students will have all the Decoding Flashcards available to them in an envelope or small plastic bag. The teacher may choose to focus on a few strategies at a time and have students work with only those particular cards until all the strategies have been introduced.)

The Decoding Flashcards can be used in various ways:

- **Shared Reading**
  As the teacher models a strategy(ies), the students can each identify the modeled strategy and hold up the appropriate flashcard(s). To help the students realize that good readers use multiple strategies, the teacher will model trying several different strategies until one works.

- **Guided Reading**
  Periodically, the teacher may ask the students to locate a place in their text, where they needed to use a decoding strategy. Each student demonstrates and explains to the group the strategy(ies) attempted. The Decoding Flashcards are used to identify the strategy(ies), as the group listens and coaches.

- **Partner Reading**
  The above practice may also be used with partners using the **RallyCoach** structure.

Decoding Strategy Graph (p. 265)

The Decoding Strategy Graph provides an additional practice opportunity that allows students to compare strategies used frequently to those that might need strengthening. The graph can be used with the **RallyCoach** structure. Students mark each time they or a partner uses a specific decoding strategy while reading.

Resources/Materials Descriptions (continued)

Fluency Student Bookmarks (p. 266)

Fluency is automatic and accurate recognition of words in a text while using phrasing and expression in a way that makes reading sound like spoken language. The Fluency Bookmark is a visual prompting tool for students to use as they learn and practice the components of fluent reading.

Fluency Graphics/Note Taking (p. 267)

The fluency page provides flexible instructional uses. The teacher may have students attach their own labels, graphics, or notes to build mental connections as they become fluent readers.

Fluency Rubrics and Graphs (pp. 271–274)

The broad fluency components of expression, phrasing, rate, and accuracy have been defined through the rubric continuum to increase students' fluency knowledge, self-awareness, and monitoring of progress.

Students must be given opportunities to reread and practice if fluency is going to improve. The graph below each rubric provides students with a visual record for charting their own progress as they practice with a partner or individually.

Together, these two tools provide data for reflection and conversation between students and between student and teacher.

Fluency Continuum (p. 275)

After using the Rubrics and Graphs described above to create a solid understanding of fluency, the Fluency Continuum becomes another self-monitoring option for students.

Fluency Resources

Decoding Strategy Bookmarks	Decoding Strategy Bookmarks
Does it make sense? Does it sound right? Does it look right?	Does it make sense? Does it sound right? Does it look right?
Picture Clues	Picture Clues
Mouth Ready	Mouth Ready
Patterns (Chunks)	Patterns (Chunks)
Reread. Fix.	Reread. Fix.
Skip word. Get clues. Reread.	Skip word. Get clues. Reread.
Think about what word makes sense.	Think about what word makes sense.
Stretch through word.	Stretch through word.
Try vowel both ways. a e i o u	Try vowel both ways. a e i o u

Balanced Literacy • First Grade • Skidmore & Graber
Kagan Publishing • 1 (800) 933-2667 • www.KaganOnline.com

Picture Clues

Mouth Ready

Pattern (Chunk)

Reread. Fix.

Skip word.
Get clues.
Reread.

Think about
what word
makes sense.

Stretch through
the word.

Try vowel both
ways.

Does it make sense?	Does it sound right?	Does it look right?

Decoding Strategy Graph

	I use picture clues.	I get my mouth ready.	I know something about the word. (chunking/patterns)	I reread. I fix.	I skip the word, get clues, reread.	I think about what word makes sense.	I stretch through the word.	I try the vowel both ways.	Does it make sense? Does it sound right? Does it look right?
12									
11									
10									
9									
8									
7									
6									
5									
4									
3									
2									
1									

Fluency
Expression

expression
- stress
- pitch
- volume
- clarity

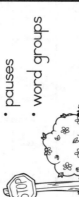

phrasing
- pauses
- word groups

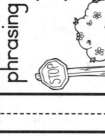

rate
- speed (just right)

accuracy
- right words
- correct pronunciation

Fluency
Expression

expression
- stress
- pitch
- volume
- clarity

phrasing
- pauses
- word groups

rate
- speed (just right)

accuracy
- right words
- correct pronunciation

Fluency
Expression

expression
- stress
- pitch
- volume
- clarity

phrasing
- pauses
- word groups

rate
- speed (just right)

accuracy
- right words
- correct pronunciation

Fluency
Expression

expression
- stress
- pitch
- volume
- clarity

phrasing
- pauses
- word groups

rate
- speed (just right)

accuracy
- right words
- correct pronunciation

Fluency Graphics/Note Taking

Instructions: Copy for each student.

Fluency Graphics/Note Taking	Fluency Graphics/Note Taking
expression  • stress • pitch • volume • clarity	
phrasing  • pauses • word groups	
rate  • speed (just right)	
accuracy  • right words • correct pronunciation	

Fluency
Activities

Activity

Fluency Scoring

Students read a text passage to a partner. The partner uses a rubric to score the reading on one dimension. Students practice reading the same passage to improve their fluency and chart their progress.

Activity Steps

1. There are four rubrics provided to work on different dimensions of fluency. Each student receives a rubric sheet.

2. Partner A reads the text passage while Partner B listens carefully, paying special attention to the rubric scoring.

3. Partner B uses the rubric to score Partner A's reading. Partner B colors in the score in the "1st time" column of the graph. Then Partner B describes the score and how Partner A can improve.

4. Partner B then reads while Partner A listens.

5. Partner A scores the reading by filling in the graph and provides feedback to Partner B.

6. The process is repeated multiple times with the same text passage to improve fluency. There are 5 columns on the graph provided so students can graph their progress.

STRUCTURE
RallyCoach

Hint:
Tell students in advance that they will be scoring each other on their reading. The scores are used only as a way for students to provide each other constructive feedback and chart their progress.

Blacklines

Expression Rubric
RallyCoach

Instructions: Copy for each student.

Score	1	2	3	4
Expression • Stress • Pitch • Volume • Clarity	No Voice change	Voice changes sometimes	Voice changes most of the time when needed	Voice changes when needed

Expression Graph
RallyCoach

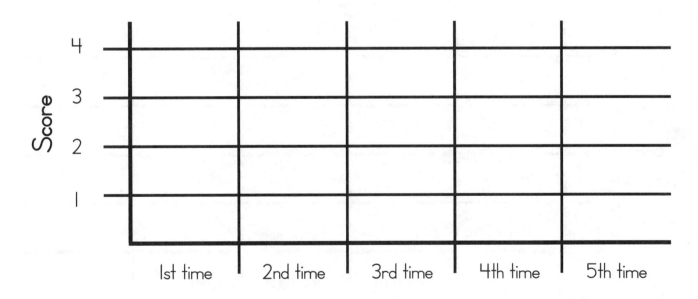

Name _____

Phrasing Rubric
RallyCoach

Instructions: Copy for each student.

Score	1	2	3	4
Phrasing • Pauses • Word Groups	Reads word by word and does not stop at punctuation	Reads in small chunks and sometimes stops at punctuation	Reads in larger chunks and usually stops at punctuation	Reads in long chunks and stops at punctuation

Phrasing Graph
RallyCoach

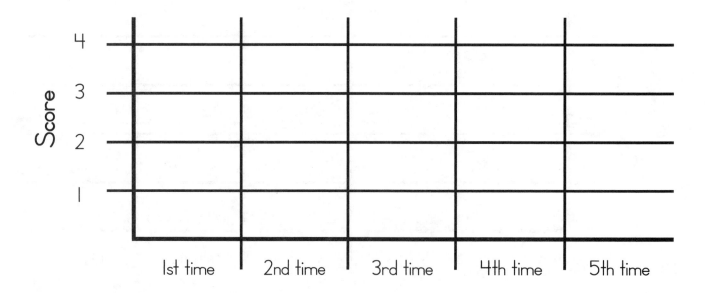

Name _____

Accuracy Rubric
RallyCoach

Instructions: Copy for each student.

Score	1	2	3	4
Accuracy • Right Words • Correct Pronunciation	Many errors	Errors, which sometimes change the meaning	Some errors, which do not change the meaning	Very few or no errors Words correctly pronounced

Accuracy Graph
RallyCoach

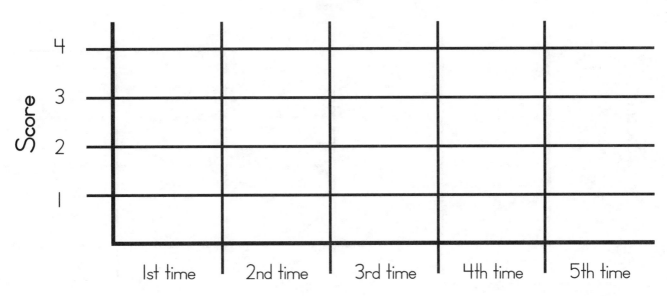

Name _____

Rate Rubric
RallyCoach

Instructions: Copy for each student.

Score	1	2	3	4
Rate • Speed (Just Right)	Reads too fast or too slow Hard to understand	Reads too fast or too slow sometimes	Reads "just right" most of the time	Keeps speed steady and "just right"

Rate Graph
RallyCoach

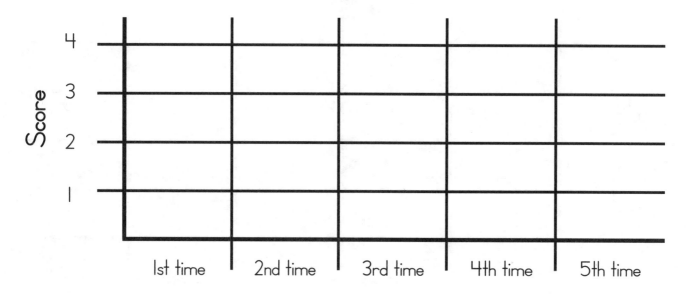

Name _____

Fluency Continuum
RallyCoach

Instructions: Copy for each student.

Fluency Continuum	Fluency Continuum
expression  • stress • pitch • volume • clarity	no · sometimes · most of the time · yes

Fluency Continuum	Fluency Continuum
phrasing  • pauses • word groups	no · sometimes · most of the time · yes

Fluency Continuum	Fluency Continuum
rate  • speed (just right)	no · sometimes · most of the time · yes

Fluency Continuum	Fluency Continuum
accuracy  • right words • correct pronunciation	no · sometimes · most of the time · yes

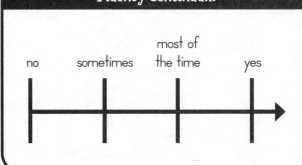
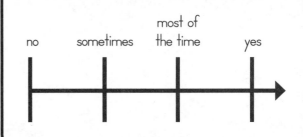

Activities

Fluency Poems

Partners present a poem—recited at times by one partner, the other partner, or both.

Activity Steps

1. The teacher provides students a poem. The poem has some lines labeled "A," some lines labeled "B," and some lines labeled, "AB." The teacher assigns pairs.

2. Pairs practice their poems. Partner A reads the A lines. Partner B reads the B lines. They read the AB lines in unison. Students listen carefully to their partners to keep the flow.

3. When ready, pairs read their poem to another pair.

Note:
A blank form is provided for creating additional Poems for Two Voices.

STRUCTURE
Poems for Two Voices

Blacklines

Hiding From the Rain

Poems for Two Voices

Instructions: Copy for each student or pair.

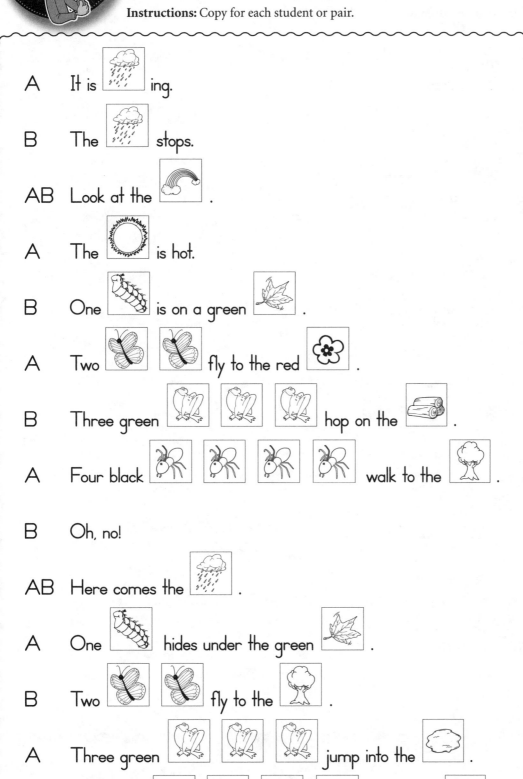

A   It is [rain]ing.

B   The [rain] stops.

AB   Look at the [rainbow].

A   The [sun] is hot.

B   One [caterpillar] is on a green [leaf].

A   Two [butterflies] fly to the red [flower].

B   Three green [frogs] hop on the [log].

A   Four black [ants] walk to the [tree].

B   Oh, no!

AB   Here comes the [rain].

A   One [caterpillar] hides under the green [leaf].

B   Two [butterflies] fly to the [tree].

A   Three green [frogs] jump into the [puddle].

B   Four black [ants] hide in the [grass].

Rhyme Time
Poems for Two Voices

Instructions: Copy for each student or pair.

A   Does a buzz in a ?

B   Yes.

B   Can a drive a ?

A   No.

A   Can a eat a ?

B   Maybe.

B   Can a sit on a ?

A   Yes, it can.

A   Will a hide in a ?

B   No.

B   Can a  wear a ?

A   No way!

Balanced Literacy • First Grade • Skidmore & Graber
Kagan Publishing • 1 (800) 933-2667 • www.KaganOnline.com

Rhyme Time

Poems for Two Voices

Instructions: Copy for each student or pair.

A   Can a  hide under the ____ ?

B   It can.

AB   Now try this . . .

A   Does the ____ have a ____ ?

B   Can a ____ be on a ____ ?

Blank Form

Poems for Two Voices

Names: _____

_____

Our Poem Is About: _____

Instructions: Copy for each pair of students.

A _____

B _____

A _____

B _____

AB _____

A _____

B _____

A _____

B _____

AB _____

Fluency

To practice sight words, phrases, and sentences, students quiz a partner, get quizzed by a partner, and then trade cards to repeat the process with a new partner.

STRUCTURE

Quiz-Quiz-Trade

Activity Steps

1 Each student receives a card with a question or direction on the front and answer on the back.

2 All students stand up, put a hand up, and pair up.

3 Partner A quizzes Partner B.

4 Partner B answers.

5 Partner A checks the answer on back and praises or coaches.

6 Partners switch roles and quiz again.

7 After they have quizzed both ways, partners trade cards, and raise their hands to find a new partner. The partner quizzing and trading proceeds for numerous pairings.

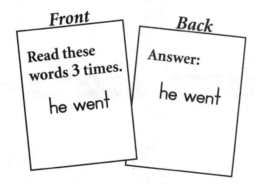

Front

Read these words 3 times.

he went

Back

Answer:

he went

Blackline

Sight Word Practice
Quiz-Quiz-Trade

Instructions: Copy enough cards so each student has one card. Cut on dotted lines and fold in half.

Sight Words	Sight Words
Question: Can you read this word? **help**	Answer: **help**
Question: Can you read this word? **are**	Answer: **are**
Question: Can you read this word? **my**	Answer: **my**
Question: Can you read this word? **little**	Answer: **little**
Question: Can you read this word? **here**	Answer: **here**

Sight Word Practice
Quiz-Quiz-Trade

Instructions: Copy enough cards so each student has one card. Cut on dotted lines and fold in half.

Sight Words	Sight Words
Question: Can you read this word? **play**	Answer: **play**
Question: Can you read this word? **my**	Answer: **my**
Question: Can you read this word? **me**	Answer: **me**
Question: Can you read this word? **said**	Answer: **said**
Question: Can you read this word? **down**	Answer: **down**

Sight Word Practice
Quiz-Quiz-Trade

Instructions: Copy enough cards so each student has one card. Cut on dotted lines and fold in half.

Sight Words	Sight Words
Question: Can you read this word? **run**	Answer: **run**
Question: Can you read this word? **not**	Answer: **not**
Question: Can you read this word? **like**	Answer: **like**
Question: Can you read this word? **will**	Answer: **will**
Question: Can you read this word? **with**	Answer: **with**

Sight Word Practice
Quiz-Quiz-Trade

Instructions: Copy enough cards so each student has one card. Cut on dotted lines and fold in half.

Sight Words	Sight Words
Question: Can you read this word?	Answer:
at	**at**

Sight Words	Sight Words
Question: Can you read this word?	Answer:
and	**and**

Sight Words	Sight Words
Question: Can you read this word?	Answer:
you	**you**

Sight Words	Sight Words
Question: Can you read this word?	Answer:
see	**see**

Sight Words	Sight Words
Question: Can you read this word?	Answer:
jump	**jump**

Sight Word Practice
Quiz-Quiz-Trade

Instructions: Copy enough cards so each student has one card. Cut on dotted lines and fold in half.

Sight Words	Sight Words
Question: Can you read this word?	Answer:
can	**can**

Sight Words	Sight Words
Question: Can you read this word?	Answer:
the	**the**

Sight Words	Sight Words
Question: Can you read this word?	Answer:
is	**is**

Sight Words	Sight Words
Question: Can you read this word?	Answer:
big	**big**

Sight Words	Sight Words
Question: Can you read this word?	Answer:
look	**look**

Fluency Word Phrases
Quiz-Quiz-Trade

Instructions: Copy enough cards so each student has one card. Cut on dotted lines and fold in half.

Fluency Word Phrases	Fluency Word Phrases
Read these words 3 times. **he went**	Answer: (Read 3 times.) **he went**
Read these words 3 times. **are you**	Answer: (Read 3 times.) **are you**
Read these words 3 times. **and his**	Answer: (Read 3 times.) **and his**
Read these words 3 times. **is a**	Answer: (Read 3 times.) **is a**

Fluency Word Phrases
Quiz-Quiz-Trade

Instructions: Copy enough cards so each student has one card. Cut on dotted lines and fold in half.

Fluency Word Phrases	Fluency Word Phrases
Read these words 3 times. **of a**	Answer: (Read 3 times.) **of a**
Read these words 3 times. **with his**	Answer: (Read 3 times.) **with his**
Read these words 3 times. **up the**	Answer: (Read 3 times.) **up the**
Read these words 3 times. **one day**	Answer: (Read 3 times.) **one day**

Fluency Word Phrases
Quiz-Quiz-Trade

Instructions: Copy enough cards so each student has one card. Cut on dotted lines and fold in half.

Fluency Word Phrases	Fluency Word Phrases
Read these words 3 times. **did you**	Answer: (Read 3 times.) **did you**
Read these words 3 times. **go down**	Answer: (Read 3 times.) **go down**
Read these words 3 times. **look up**	Answer: (Read 3 times.) **look up**
Read these words 3 times. **come here**	Answer: (Read 3 times.) **come here**

Fluency Word Phrases
Quiz-Quiz-Trade

Instructions: Copy enough cards so each student has one card. Cut on dotted lines and fold in half.

Fluency Word Phrases	Fluency Word Phrases
Read these words 3 times. **no way**	Answer: (Read 3 times.) **no way**
Read these words 3 times. **see me**	Answer: (Read 3 times.) **see me**
Read these words 3 times. **will they**	Answer: (Read 3 times.) **will they**
Read these words 3 times. **you and I**	Answer: (Read 3 times.) **you and I**

Fluency Word Phrases
Quiz-Quiz-Trade

Instructions: Copy enough cards so each student has one card. Cut on dotted lines and fold in half.

Fluency Word Phrases	Fluency Word Phrases
Read these words 3 times. ## then he	Answer: (Read 3 times.) ## then he
Read these words 3 times. ## the man	Answer: (Read 3 times.) ## the man
Read these words 3 times. ## not me	Answer: (Read 3 times.) ## not me
Read these words 3 times. ## as he	Answer: (Read 3 times.) ## as he

Fluency Word Phrases
Quiz-Quiz-Trade

Instructions: Copy enough cards so each student has one card. Cut on dotted lines and fold in half.

Fluency Word Phrases	Fluency Word Phrases
Read these words 3 times. **when the**	Answer: (Read 3 times.) **when the**
Read these words 3 times. **over the**	Answer: (Read 3 times.) **over the**
Read these words 3 times. **he could**	Answer: (Read 3 times.) **he could**
Read these words 3 times. **the other**	Answer: (Read 3 times.) **the other**

Balanced Literacy • First Grade • Skidmore & Graber
Kagan Publishing • 1 (800) 933-2667 • www.KaganOnline.com

Fluency Word Phrases
Quiz-Quiz-Trade

Instructions: Copy enough cards so each student has one card. Cut on dotted lines and fold in half.

Fluency Word Phrases	Fluency Word Phrases
Read these words 3 times. **and they**	Answer: (Read 3 times.) **and they**
Read these words 3 times. **came to**	Answer: (Read 3 times.) **came to**
Read these words 3 times. **up and**	Answer: (Read 3 times.) **up and**
Read these words 3 times. **and then**	Answer: (Read 3 times.) **and then**

Fluency Word Phrases
Quiz-Quiz-Trade

Instructions: Copy enough cards so each student has one card. Cut on dotted lines and fold in half.

Fluency Word Phrases	Fluency Word Phrases
Read these words 3 times. **down the**	Answer: (Read 3 times.) **down the**
Read these words 3 times. **they were**	Answer: (Read 3 times.) **they were**
Read these words 3 times. **going to**	Answer: (Read 3 times.) **going to**
Read these words 3 times. **you are**	Answer: (Read 3 times.) **you are**

Fluency Word Phrases
Quiz-Quiz-Trade

Instructions: Copy enough cards so each student has one card. Cut on dotted lines and fold in half.

Fluency Word Phrases	Fluency Word Phrases
Read these words 3 times. ## she was	Answer: (Read 3 times.) ## she was
Read these words 3 times. ## she said	Answer: (Read 3 times.) ## she said
Read these words 3 times. ## when he	Answer: (Read 3 times.) ## when he
Read these words 3 times. ## with the	Answer: (Read 3 times.) ## with the

Fluency Word Phrases
Quiz-Quiz-Trade

Instructions: Copy enough cards so each student has one card. Cut on dotted lines and fold in half.

Fluency Word Phrases

Read these words 3 times.

there was

Fluency Word Phrases

Answer:

(Read 3 times.)

there was

Fluency Word Phrases

Read these words 3 times.

into the

Fluency Word Phrases

Answer:

(Read 3 times.)

into the

Fluency Word Phrases

Read these words 3 times.

from the

Fluency Word Phrases

Answer:

(Read 3 times.)

from the

Fluency Word Phrases

Read these words 3 times.

said the

Fluency Word Phrases

Answer:

(Read 3 times.)

said the

 Balanced Literacy • First Grade • Skidmore & Graber
Kagan Publishing • 1 (800) 933-2667 • www.KaganOnline.com

Fluency Sentences
Quiz-Quiz-Trade

Instructions: Copy enough cards so each student has one card. Cut on dotted lines and fold in half.

Fluency Sentences	Fluency Sentences
Read this sentence. Remember phrasing and expression. "I love to swing!" said Pat.	Answer: "I love to swing!" said Pat.
Read this sentence. Remember phrasing and expression. "Don't look at me!" screamed Mary.	Answer: "Don't look at me!" screamed Mary.
Read this sentence. Remember phrasing and expression. Sam has a pet dog, cat, fish, and hamster.	Answer: Sam has a pet dog, cat, fish, and hamster.
Read this sentence. Remember phrasing and expression. "Look at that BIG dog!" shouted Bret.	Answer: "Look at that BIG dog!" shouted Bret.

Fluency Sentences
Quiz-Quiz-Trade

Instructions: Copy enough cards so each student has one card. Cut on dotted lines and fold in half.

Fluency Sentences	Fluency Sentences
Read this sentence. Remember phrasing and expression. "My birthday is today!"	Answer: "My birthday is today!"
Read this sentence. Remember phrasing and expression. The dog has five puppies.	Answer: The dog has five puppies.
Read this sentence. Remember phrasing and expression. Red, green, and yellow are the colors I like.	Answer: Red, green, and yellow are the colors I like.
Read this sentence. Remember phrasing and expression. Alex cried, "I want to go home NOW!"	Answer: Alex cried, "I want to go home NOW!"

Fluency Sentences
Quiz-Quiz-Trade

Instructions: Copy enough cards so each student has one card. Cut on dotted lines and fold in half.

Fluency Sentences

Read this sentence. Remember phrasing and expression.

Cats, goats, cows, and rats are mammals.

Fluency Sentences

Answer:

Cats, goats, cows, and rats are mammals.

Fluency Sentences

Read this sentence. Remember phrasing and expression.

"Yes! Yes! Yes! We get to go swimming!"

Fluency Sentences

Answer:

"Yes! Yes! Yes! We get to go swimming!"

Fluency Sentences

Read this sentence. Remember phrasing and expression.

Sea otters eat clams and other shellfish.

Fluency Sentences

Answer:

Sea otters eat clams and other shellfish.

Fluency Sentences

Read this sentence. Remember phrasing and expression.

"I like to hop! I like to skip!"

Fluency Sentences

Answer:

"I like to hop! I like to skip!"

Fluency Sentences
Quiz-Quiz-Trade

Instructions: Copy enough cards so each student has one card. Cut on dotted lines and fold in half.

Fluency Sentences Read this sentence. Remember phrasing and expression. Run, mice, run!	**Fluency Sentences** Answer: Run, mice, run!
Fluency Sentences Read this sentence. Remember phrasing and expression. "How old are you?" I asked my friend.	**Fluency Sentences** Answer: "How old are you?" I asked my friend.
Fluency Sentences Read this sentence. Remember phrasing and expression. Jeff asked, "Who took my lunch?"	**Fluency Sentences** Answer: Jeff asked, "Who took my lunch?"
Fluency Sentences Read this sentence. Remember phrasing and expression. Bob, Jane, Beth, and Jill will be at my party.	**Fluency Sentences** Answer: Bob, Jane, Beth, and Jill will be at my party.

Fluency Sentences
Quiz-Quiz-Trade

Instructions: Copy enough cards so each student has one card. Cut on dotted lines and fold in half.

Fluency Sentences	Fluency Sentences
Read this sentence. Remember phrasing and expression. "I want to eat NOW!"	Answer: "I want to eat NOW!"
Read this sentence. Remember phrasing and expression. Joe whispered, "Are you as scared as I am?"	Answer: Joe whispered, "Are you as scared as I am?"
Read this sentence. Remember phrasing and expression. "I'm going to bed," yawned John sleepily.	Answer: "I'm going to bed," yawned John sleepily.
Read this sentence. Remember phrasing and expression. We have a new boy in our class.	Answer: We have a new boy in our class.

Fluency Sentences
Quiz-Quiz-Trade

Instructions: Copy enough cards so each student has one card. Cut on dotted lines and fold in half.

Fluency Sentences	Fluency Sentences
Read this sentence. Remember phrasing and expression. "How are you?" "I am fine."	Answer: "How are you?" "I am fine."
Read this sentence. Remember phrasing and expression. "One, two, three, look at me," said the teacher.	Answer: "One, two, three, look at me," said the teacher.
Read this sentence. Remember phrasing and expression. "BOOOO!" said the goblin on Halloween night.	Answer: "BOOOO!" said the goblin on Halloween night.
Read this sentence. Remember phrasing and expression. "Ribbit, ribbit," croaked the frog to the toad.	Answer: "Ribbit, ribbit," croaked the frog to the toad.

Fluency Sentences
Quiz-Quiz-Trade

Instructions: Copy enough cards so each student has one card. Cut on dotted lines and fold in half.

Fluency Sentences	Fluency Sentences
Read this sentence. Remember phrasing and expression. I can come to your house to play today.	Answer: I can come to your house to play today.
Read this sentence. Remember phrasing and expression. "Me-ow," cried the hungry kitty.	Answer: "Me-ow," cried the hungry kitty.
Read this sentence. Remember phrasing and expression. "Be quiet! Don't let anyone hear us."	Answer: "Be quiet! Don't let anyone hear us."
Read this sentence. Remember phrasing and expression. I am going on a trip in three days.	Answer: I am going on a trip in three days.

Fluency Sentences
Quiz-Quiz-Trade

Instructions: Copy enough cards so each student has one card. Cut on dotted lines and fold in half.

Fluency Sentences	Fluency Sentences
Read this sentence. Remember phrasing and expression. "I love candy!" said my dad.	Answer: "I love candy!" said my dad.
Read this sentence. Remember phrasing and expression. You are too little to come with me.	Answer: You are too little to come with me.
Read this sentence. Remember phrasing and expression. The sheep cried, "Baa-baa."	Answer: The sheep cried, "Baa-baa."
Read this sentence. Remember phrasing and expression. I am looking for my lost shoe.	Answer: I am looking for my lost shoe.

Punctuation Showdown

Teams play Showdown to practice correct ending punctuation.

STRUCTURE

Showdown

Note:
The teacher is the
Showdown Captain,
rather than rotating the
responsibility among the
team. This activity can also
be done with partners.

Activity Steps

1. Each team receives a Team Set of cards. If the teacher is the Showdown Captain, make one overhead transparency in place of Team cards. Every student receives a Student Set of cards.

2. The Team Set is placed facedown in the middle of the team. Or, if the teacher is the Showdown Captain, one card is placed on the overhead at a time. Students hold their Student Set in their hands.

3. The teacher is the Showdown Captain or selects one student to be the Showdown Captain for the first round.

4. The Showdown Captain (teacher) selects the top card from the middle and reads it aloud.

5. Working alone, students individually identify an answer from their card set.

6. When finished, teammates signal they are ready.

7. The Showdown Captain (teacher) calls, "Showdown!"

8. Teammates show their answers at the same time.

9. The Showdown Captain (teacher) leads checking.

10. If correct, the team celebrates. If not, the teammates coach, then celebrate.

11. The person to the left of the Showdown Captain becomes the Showdown Captain for the next round. Or, the teacher continues as Showdown Captain.

Blacklines

Ending Punctuation (.?)

Showdown (Teacher Transparency)

Note: Teacher makes one transparency copy, or one set of sentence strips per pair or team.

Do you have a pet at home ☐

When is your birthday ☐

I like to eat at McDonald's ☐

Where is the bus taking us ☐

What is your favorite movie ☐

My family is going to the park ☐

Can you skate ☐

I am going fishing on Saturday ☐

He will play with you today ☐

May I go to the zoo ☐

Ending Punctuation (.?)
Showdown (Student Set)

Note: Each player needs two cards: . and ?

Ending Punctuation Showdown—Student Set	Ending Punctuation Showdown—Student Set	Ending Punctuation Showdown—Student Set	Ending Punctuation Showdown—Student Set
.	?	.	?
Ending Punctuation Showdown—Student Set	Ending Punctuation Showdown—Student Set	Ending Punctuation Showdown—Student Set	Ending Punctuation Showdown—Student Set
.	?	.	?

Ending Punctuation (. ? !)
Showdown (Teacher Transparency)

Instructions: Teacher makes one transparency copy, or one set of sentence strips per pair or team.

Al and Kim are in school ☐

What is your name ☐

Is that your pet cat ☐

Help me, I have fallen ☐

Ted is a friend of mine ☐

Watch out for that big hole ☐

My cat is eating ☐

Will you help me read this book ☐

Ouch, something is biting my leg ☐

I will take my dog for a walk ☐

Ending Punctuation (.?!)
Showdown (Student Set)

Note: Each player needs three cards: . ? and !

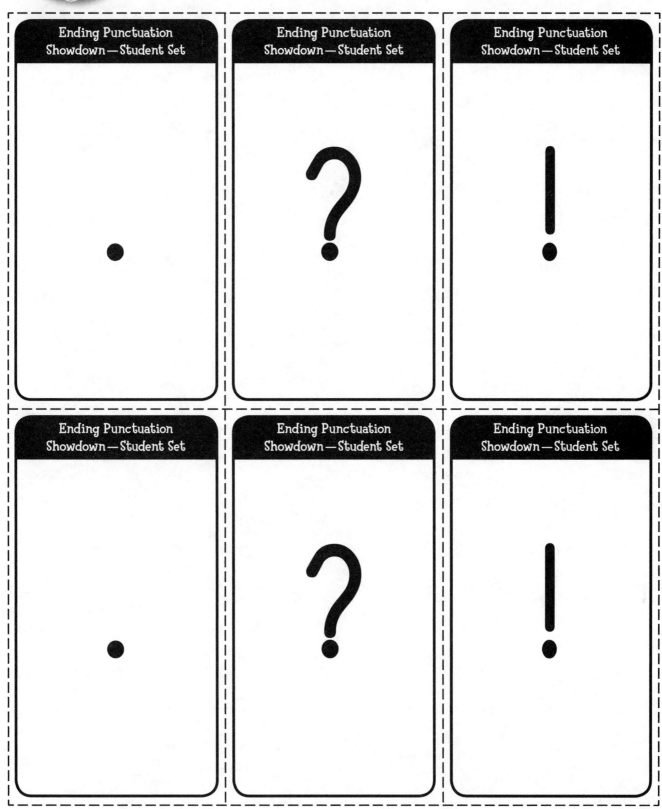

Ending Punctuation
Showdown—Student Set

.

Ending Punctuation
Showdown—Student Set

?

Ending Punctuation
Showdown—Student Set

!

Ending Punctuation
Showdown—Student Set

.

Ending Punctuation
Showdown—Student Set

?

Ending Punctuation
Showdown—Student Set

!

Balanced Literacy

Comprehension

Word Study

Fluency

Writing

Writing

Writing Overview

Authors use four main text types to convey meaning in print:

- **Narrative**—to entertain
- **Expository**—to inform
- **Technical**—to tell how to...
- **Persuasive**—to convince

Expository writing is a great starting place for students. Children naturally write in expository form, informing us of what they know or are learning from their experiences. Writing and reading are reciprocal processes, each supporting the other. Understanding why and how authors use text features helps students apply these same organizational features in their own writing.

Note:

The teacher should have his or her own photograph/picture and an ongoing piece of writing that is used for modeling in each lesson.

Balanced Literacy • First Grade • Skidmore & Graber
Kagan Publishing • 1 (800) 933-2667 • www.KaganOnline.com

Table of Writing Resources

Page(s)	Resources	Balanced Literacy				
		Aloud	Shared	Guided	Independent	Literature Circles
318	**Expository Writing Resources/Materials Descriptions**					
319–321	**Types of Words**	●	●	●	●	
322	**Six Trait Questions**	●	●	●	●	
323–328	**Six Trait Question Strips**	●	●	●	●	

Table of Writing Activities

Page(s)	Six Traits	Structures	Activities	Resources
332	Ideas			
333–334		• Timed Pair Share	Emotion Words	
335–336		• StandUp–HandUp–PairUp • RallyRobin	Prewriting	
337	Word Choice			
338		• RallyRobin	Creating Description Chart • Day 1 • Day 2	
339–340		• RallyRobin • Timed Pair Share	Writing Descriptions	
341–343		• StandUp–HandUp–PairUp • Timed Pair Share • RallyCoach	Listing and Writing Action Words	• Six Trait Question Strip—Word Choice • Shared Writing Example
344–345		• StandUp–HandUp–PairUp • Timed Pair Share • RallyCoach	Listing and Writing Describing Words	• Six Trait Question Strip—Word Choice
346–350		• RallyRobin	Choosing Action, Naming, and Describing Words/ Forming Sentences	• Shared Writing Example • Word Choice Picture Cards

Table of Writing Activities (continued)

Page(s)	Six Traits	Structures	Activities	Resources
351	Organization			
352–354		• RallyCoach	Hooks	• Hook Examples • Shared Writing Example
355	Conventions			
356–360		• RallyCoach	Puncutation and Capitalization	• Sentence Strips • Blank Form for Sentence Punctuation and Capitalization
361–362		• Mix-Pair-Share	Checking My Writing/Sharing of Student Work	• Six Trait Self-Assessment • Checking My Writing
363		• Mix-Pair-Share	Sharing Student Work	

Writing Resources

Expository Writing Resources

Resources/Materials Descriptions

Students choose a photograph to use as the focus for their writing. Each student has his or her own photograph. Photographs could be of individual students engaged in an activity, that they would like to write about (playing soccer at recess, reading, climbing on a jungle gym, eating lunch, getting on the bus, etc.) The photographs need to show action and details, which will allow for more powerful writing.

One key to scaffolding instruction is the inclusion of modeling. **The teacher should have his or her own photograph and ongoing piece of writing that are used for modeling in each lesson.** This permits the students to see the skill being used, creates a better understanding of what is expected, and allows for more effective application of the skill.

Types of Words: (pp. 319–321)
These three pages give examples of action words, naming words, and describing words. They are a resource that can be made into overhead transparencies or enlarged and used as posters.

Six Trait Questions (p. 322)
This page is a teacher resource listing the six traits and questions for each trait to help students focus as they are writing.

Six Trait Question Strips (pp. 323–328)
Each trait and two easy-to-understand questions that reinforce the trait have been made into question strips that can be used for classroom wall displays, overhead transparencies, and/or individually held up next to the teacher's enlarged writing text. During this shared writing time, the students can focus their attention on the teacher as she or he writes, answers the questions, and makes additions to the text. The individual question strips allow the teacher to scaffold the instruction by concentrating on one or two traits at a time. Students will soon understand that answering "yes" to the questions given for each trait will not only strengthen the writer's skill, but will also increase the reader's engagement as they read the piece.

Action Words
Types of Words

(Words telling what someone or something is doing)

push

run

hit

read

hop

buzz

nap

Naming Words
Types of Words

(Words given to people, things, animals, or places)

house

girl

sun

umbrella

friends

butterfly

books

playground

Describing Words
Types of Words

(Words telling something about the naming word.)

size (tall, short)

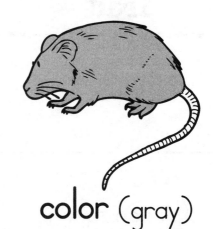

color (gray)

shape (round)

texture-feel (prickly)

number (three)

Six Trait Questions
Teacher Resources

Trait	Question
Ideas	• Do I like my topic? • Does my writing make sense when I read it?
Organization	• Did I use a hook at the beginning? • Does my writing have a good ending?
Voice	• Does my writing tell the reader how I feel? • Did I use some sentences that can be read with expression?
Word Choice	• Did I use strong action words? • Did I use describing words?
Sentence Fluency	• Is my paper easy to read? • Do my sentences start with different words?
Conventions	• Does each sentence begin with a capital? • Does each sentence end with punctuation?

Six Trait Question Strips

Ideas

Adapted from Six Trait Writing Model: NWREL (Northwest Regional Educational Lab)

Ideas

Do I like my topic?

Ideas

Does my writing make sense when I read it?

Six Trait Question Strips
Organization

Adapted from Six Trait Writing Model: NWREL (Northwest Regional Educational Lab)

Organization

Did I use a hook at the beginning?

Organization

Does my writing have a good ending?

Six Trait Question Strips
Voice

Adapted from Six Trait Writing Model: NWREL (Northwest Regional Educational Lab)

Voice

Does my writing tell the reader how I feel?

Voice

Did I use some sentences that can be read with expression?

Six Trait Question Strips
Word Choice

Adapted from Six Trait Writing Model: NWREL (Northwest Regional Educational Lab)

Word Choice

Did I use strong action words?

Word Choice

Did I use describing words?

□ color □ size □ shape

□ texture □ number

Six Trait Question Strips
Sentence Fluency

Adapted from Six Trait Writing Model: NWREL (Northwest Regional Educational Lab)

Sentence Fluency

Is my paper easy to read?

Sentence Fluency

Do my sentences start with different words?

Six Trait Question Strips
Conventions

Adapted from Six Trait Writing Model: NWREL (Northwest Regional Educational Lab)

Conventions

Does each sentence begin with a capital?

Conventions

Does each sentence end with punctuation?

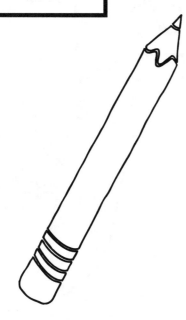

Balanced Literacy • First Grade • Skidmore & Graber
Kagan Publishing • 1 (800) 933-2667 • www.KaganOnline.com

Writing
Activities

Writing Activities

Shared writing is a powerful instructional component of balanced literacy. The following lessons are guides for the teacher to use to introduce the skill. Shared writing lets the students observe the skill being implemented into authentic writing. With this understanding and the practice opportunities provided in the lessons, students will be better equipped to integrate the skills into their own writing.

Page(s)	Six Traits	Structures	Activities	Resources
332	Ideas			
333–334		Timed Pair Share	Ideas Emotion Words	
335–336		StandUp–HandUp–PairUp and RallyRobin	Prewriting	
337	Word Choice			
338		RallyRobin	Creating Description Chart • Day 1 • Day 2	
339–340		RallyRobin and Timed Pair Share	Writing Descriptions	
341–343		StandUp–HandUp–PairUp and Timed Pair Share and RallyCoach	Listing and Writing Action Words	• Six Trait Question Strips—Word Choice • Shared Writing Example
344–346		StandUp–HandUp–PairUp and Timed Pair Share and RallyCoach	Listing and Writing Describing Words	• Six Trait Question Strips—Word Choice • Shared Writing Example

Writing Activities
(continued)

Page(s)	Six Traits	Structures	Activities	Resources
347–350		RallyRobin	Choosing Action, Naming, and Describing Words/ Forming Sentences	• Word Choice Picture Cards
351	Organization			
352–354		RallyCoach	Hooks	• Hook Examples • Shared Writing Example
355	Conventions			
356–360		RallyCoach	Punctuation and Capitalization	• Sentence Strips • Blank Form for Sentence Punctuation and Capitalization
361–362			Checking My Writing/Sharing of Student Work	• Checking My Writing
363		Mix-Pair-Share	Sharing Student Work	

Ideas

- Do I like my topic?

- Does my writing make sense when I read it?

Ideas
Emotion Words
(pp. 333–334)

Students generate a list of writing possibilities for future reference.
<u>*Note:*</u> *The activities on pages 333–334 are <u>NOT</u> directly tied to the following lessons.*

Setup

- *poster labeled with magazine cutout pictures of facial expressions or photographs of students depicting each emotion*

A class discussion is held about situations for each emotion. The teacher writes a few example statements under each emotion. The students can use this class chart to help them choose ideas to write about when they are stuck. Another option is to have each student create an individual chart for his or her own use.

happy	sad	surprised	angry	puzzled
-going to a movie	-rainy day	-Grandma's visit	-friend tattled	-lost library book
-slumber party	-pet ran away	-new student	-stolen bike	-science experiment
-zoo trip	-broke my arm	-winning soccer game		

Ideas
Emotion Words
(pp. 333–334)

Partners take timed turns listening and sharing.

Students generate a list of writing possibilities for future reference. A class discussion is held about situations for each emotion.

Setup

- *poster labeled with magazine cutout pictures of facial expressions or photographs of students depicting each emotion*
- *writing paper*

STRUCTURE

Timed Pair Share

Activity Steps

1. Teacher identifies an emotion from the chart and states how long each student will have to share about his/her personal experience.

2. Teacher provides think time.

3. In pairs, Partner A shares; Partner B listens.

4. Partner B responds.

5. Partners switch roles.

   * *Students return to their seats to write.*

Variation

- *The teacher may repeat Steps 3 through 5 to allow students to generate more than one idea for the chosen emotion. Students will then choose one of the situations to write about.*
- *After going through all the emotions, the teacher may choose two different emotions for Timed Pair Share allowing more writing choices for students.*
- *As the year progresses, the teacher may add additional emotions to the chart.*

Ideas
Prewriting
(pp. 335–336)

Students stand up, put their hands up, and quickly find a partner.

Setup

- *Individuals have previously been given opportunity to choose a picture and have spent some individual focused think time—"What do you notice about your picture?" "What is happening in your picture?"*
- *Individuals take the chosen picture with them, as they move to new partners.*

Activity Steps

1. Teacher says, "StandUp–HandUp–PairUp!
2. Students stand up and keep one hand in the air until they find the closest partner who's not a teammate.
3. Partners share using **RallyRobin.**
4. Continue from Step 1.

STRUCTURE
StandUp-HandUp-PairUp

Ideas
Prewriting
(pp. 335–336)

In pairs, students alternate generating oral responses. Time spent orally generating complete thoughts improves the quality of writing.

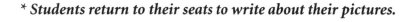

Activity Steps

1. Teacher gives think time for pairs to study Partner A's picture.

2. Teacher says, "Take turns sharing what is happening in Partner A's picture."

3. In pairs, students take turns sharing responses, until teacher calls time.

4. Teacher gives think time for pairs to study Partner B's picture.

5. Teacher says, "Take turns sharing what is happening in Partner B's picture."

6. In pairs, students take turns sharing responses, until teacher calls time.

STRUCTURE
RallyRobin

* Students return to their seats to write about their pictures.

Word Choice

• Did I use strong action words?

• Did I use describing words?

☐ color   ☐ size   ☐ shape

☐ texture   ☐ number

Word Choice
Creating Description Chart
(pp. 338)

In pairs, students alternate generating oral responses.

The teacher and students create a Description Chart to be used as a classroom reference to reinforce word choice.

Activity Steps: Day 1

1. Teacher holds up and passes around an object.

2. In pairs, students take turns orally listing describing words for the object.

   • *The teacher makes a list on chart paper as the class orally shares words.*

3. Repeat Steps 1 and 2 for several more objects.

STRUCTURE
RallyRobin

Setup: Day 1

- *two or three objects*
- *chart paper*

Activity Steps: Day 2

1. Prior to this lesson, the teacher writes each word from the list on a separate card.

2. Display all word cards (tape to chalkboard).

3. Students help group words.

4. Generate headings for categories.

5. Explain that these words are describing words. The purpose of describing words is to create a picture in the mind of the reader.

6. The chart is displayed in the room as a writing reference.

Setup: Day2

- *blank word cards or index cards*
- *chart paper*

size	color	shape	texture (feels like)	number
giant miniature	aqua crimson	oval straight	silky rough	one hundred twenty
_____	_____	_____	_____	_____

Word Choice
Writing Descriptions
(pp. 339–340)

In pairs, students alternate generating oral responses.

Students generate describing words for a stuffed animal.

Setup

- **one stuffed animal**
- **chart paper**

STRUCTURE
RallyRobin

Activity Steps

- *Teacher uses a stuffed animal (raccoon) for her modeled writing.*

1. Students turn to their partner and orally take turns listing describing words about the animal.

- *The teacher writes a few sentences about the animal with minimal description.*

> The raccoon has a mask.
> It has a tail.
> The raccoon has claws for climbing trees.

- *The teacher has students follow along as she reads aloud sentences. She then asks them to close their eyes and think about the picture formed in their minds, as she reads the sentences again.*

Word Choice
Writing Descriptions
(pp. 339–340)

Partners take timed turns listening and sharing.

Students generate describing words to add to sentences.

Activity Steps

1. Teacher asks students to find one or two places to add a describing word in raccoon sentences and states how long each student will have to share. *(Refer to the description chart made on Day 2 of the previous word choice activity for examples of describing words, if needed.)*

2. Teacher provides think time.

3. In pairs Partner A shares; Partner B listens.

4. Partner B responds.

5. Partners switch roles.

• *The teacher adds describing words to the sentences.*

> The raccoon has a **black face** mask **over** its **eyes**.
> It has a **bushy**, **ringed** tail.
> The **quick** raccoon has **five sharp** claws for climbing **tall** trees.

• *The teacher reads aloud the sentences.*

• *The teacher has the students close their eyes, as she rereads.*

• *Students discuss how a description created a more detailed picture in their minds.*

* *Repeat the activity with each team having a different animal.*

STRUCTURE
Timed
Pair Share

Balanced Literacy • First Grade • Skidmore & Graber
Kagan Publishing • 1 (800) 933-2667 • www.KaganOnline.com

Word Choice
Listing Action Words
(pp. 341–343)

Students stand up, put their hands up, and quickly find a partner.

Action words reinforce descriptive writing, as well as keep the reader actively involved.

STRUCTURE
StandUp-HandUp-PairUp

Setup

- *The teacher takes a digital photograph of each student doing something (going down a slide, jumping rope, reading, talking to a friend, etc.) or has each child bring a home photo with him/her in it.*
- *This photograph will be used for the lessons on page 341–363.*

Activity Steps

- *Teacher models generating action words by showing his/her photograph, orally listing action words (pushing, holding, sitting).*

1. Teacher says, "Stand up, hand up, pair up!" Students take their individual photographs with them.

2. Students stand up and keep one hand in the air until they find the closest partner who's not a teammate.

3. Teacher states that students will be sharing action words about their individual photographs.

4. Teacher provides think time.

5. Partners share using **Timed Pair Share**.

Activity Steps

1. Teacher states how long partners have to share.

2. In Pairs, Partner A shares; Partner B listens.

3. Partner B responds.

4. Partners switch roles.

STRUCTURE
Timed Pair Share

Word Choice
Writing Action Words
(pp. 341–343)

Partners take turns reading their writing and coaching.

Action words reinforce descriptive writing, as well as keep the reader actively involved.

Setup

- *Chart paper with photograph attached for modeling. Six Trait Question Strip for Word Choice (Did I use strong action words?)*
- *Individual student photographs attached to writing paper*

Activity Steps

- *Teacher models several complete thoughts about the actions she sees in her photograph and uses the Six Trait Question Strips for Word Choice (Did I use strong action words?) to model checking and revising writing. The teacher rereads the sentences. Using class consensus, the action words are identified and underlined on the chart example. (See the Shared Writing Example on the following page.)*

- *The students write several complete thoughts about the action that is taking place in their photographs.*

1. Partner A reads his/her writing underlining the action words.

2. Partner B watches, listens, checks for action words, and praises.

3. Partner B reads his/her writing underlining the action words.

4. Partner A watches, listens, checks for action words, and praises.

5. Partners share using **Timed Pair Share**.

STRUCTURE
RallyCoach

Blacklines

Shared Writing Example
Word Choice–Action
RallyCoach

My dad is <u>pushing</u> me on the tire swing.

I am <u>holding</u> onto the chain.

I am <u>sitting</u> on top of the tire.

The chain is over a tree branch.

We are having fun together.

Word Choice
Listing Describing Words
(pp. 344–346)

Students stand up, put their hands up, and quickly find a partner.

Describing words help the reader form pictures in his/her mind.

Setup

- *The digital photograph of each student doing something (going down a slide, jumping rope, reading, talking to a friend, etc.) and the written sentences from the previous activities, "Word Choice—Listing Action Words and Writing Action Words" are needed.*

STRUCTURE
StandUp-HandUp-PairUp

Activity Steps

- *Teacher models generating describing words by showing her photograph and orally listing describing words (black, long, cold).*

1. Teacher says, "Stand up, hand up, pair up!" Students take their individual photographs with them.

2. Students stand up and keep one hand in the air until they find the closest partner who's not a teammate.

3. Teacher states that students will be sharing describing words about their individual photographs.

4. Teacher provides think time.

5. Partners share using **Timed Pair Share**.

Activity Steps

1. Teacher states how long partners have to share.

2. In Pairs, Partner A shares; Partner B listens.

3. Partner B responds.

4. Partners switch roles.

STRUCTURE
Timed Pair Share

Word Choice
Writing Describing Words
(pp. 344–346)

Partners take turns reading their writing and coaching.

Describing words help the reader form pictures in his/her mind.

Setup

- *Previously used photograph and modeled writing for action words*
- *Six Trait Question Strip for Word Choice (Did I use describing words? color, size, shape, texture, number)*
- *Individual student photographs attached to writing paper with their action word sentences*

STRUCTURE
RallyCoach

Activity Steps

- *Teacher models adding several describing words she sees in his or her photograph and uses the Six Trait Question Strips for Word Choice (Did I use describing words?) to model checking and revising writing. The teacher rereads the sentences. Using class consensus, the describing words are identified and circled on the chart example. (See the Shared Writing Example on page 346.)*

- *The students add several describing words to the sentences about their photographs.*

1. Partner A reads his/her writing circling the describing words.

2. Partner B watches, listens, checks for describing words, and praises.

3. Partner B reads his/her writing circling the describing words.

4. Partner A watches, listens, checks for describing words, and praises.

Blacklines

Shared Writing Example
Word Choice–Description
RallyCoach

(black)

My dad is <u>pushing</u> me on the tire swing.

(long/cold)

I am <u>holding</u> onto the chain.

(smooth)

I am <u>sitting</u> on top of the tire.

(one/strong)

The chain is over a tree branch.

We are having fun together.

Word Choice
Choosing Action, Naming, and Describing Words/Forming Sentences
(pp. 347–350)

In pairs, students alternate generating oral responses.

Students practice choosing action words, naming words, and describing words in preparation for future writing.

Setup

- *Teacher reviews action, naming, and describing words (one at a time). Refer to "Types of Words" in the Writing Resource Section.*
- *Color and cut apart picture cards on pages 348–350 or cut pictures from magazines, calendars, etc.*

STRUCTURE
RallyRobin

Variation

- *The picture cards may be used as pairs take turns sharing complete sentences about the pictures using action, naming, and describing words.*
EXAMPLE: The small boy is sitting and reading his favorite blue book.

Activity Steps

1. Pairs choose a picture card.

2. In pairs, students take turns orally listing an action word for the picture.

3. When pairs have listed as many possible action words to go with their picture as they can, they choose another picture card and continue from Step 2.

* *RallyRobin is continued using the above steps for naming words and describing words after they have been reviewed. The teacher may choose to divide describing words into categories for review and practice (size, color, shape, number, texture/feel).*

BlackLines

Word Choice Picture Cards

Action, Naming, and Describing Words
RallyRobin

 Balanced Literacy • First Grade • Skidmore & Graber
Kagan Publishing • 1 (800) 933-2667 • www.KaganOnline.com

Word Choice Picture Cards
Action, Naming, and Describing Words
RallyRobin

Word Choice Picture Cards
Action, Naming, and Describing Words
RallyRobin

Balanced Literacy • First Grade • Skidmore & Graber
Kagan Publishing • 1 (800) 933-2667 • www.KaganOnline.com

Organization

- Did I use a hook at the beginning?

- Does my writing have a good ending?

Organization
(pp. 352–354)

Partners take turns adding a beginning hook to their writing, while the other checks, coaches, and praises.

Setup

• *Individual student writing with action and describing words from previous activities*

Activity Steps

• *The teacher models adding several different beginning hooks to his/her own writing, choosing the best one. See the "Hook Examples" and the "Shared Writing Example" on the following pages.*

1. Partner A orally adds a beginning hook to his/her writing.

2. Partner B watches, listens, and praises.

3. Partner B orally adds a beginning hook to his/her writing.

4. Partner A watches, listens, and praises.

STRUCTURE
RallyCoach

Blacklines

Hook Examples
Organization
RallyCoach

question

Do you like to swing?
I sure do.

action words

I'm <u>gliding</u> and <u>flying</u>
through the air.

sound effect

<u>Whooooosh!</u>

exclamation

I love to swing!

Shared Writing Example
Organization–Beginning Hook
RallyCoach

I love to swing! (hook)

My dad is pushing me on the black tire swing.

I am holding onto the cold chain.

I am sitting on top of the smooth tire.

The chain is over a strong tree branch.

We are having fun together.

Conventions

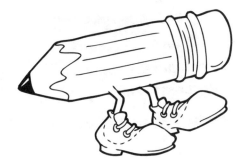

- Does each sentence begin with a capital?

- Does each sentence end with punctuation?

CONTINUOUS WRITING
Project

Conventions
(pp. 356–360)

Partners take turns, one solving a problem while the other coaches.

Setup

- *Cut-apart sentence strips with missing punctuation and beginning of sentence capitalization*
- *One colored pencil*

Variation

- *Each partner may use a different color of pencil*

Activity Steps

1. Partner A and B choose a sentence strip and read the sentence aloud together.

2. Partner A orally tells one correction or addition he/she is making and the reason why. Partner A uses a colored pencil to make the correction or addition.

3. Partner B watches and listens, checks and praises.

4. Partner B orally tells one correction or addition in the same sentence he/she is making and the reason why. Partner B uses a colored pencil to make the correction or addition.

5. Partner A watches and listens, check, and praises.

6. Repeat starting at Step 2.

7. Continue until Partner A and B agree that all possible corrections and revisions have been made.

8. Repeat starting at Step 1 by choosing a new sentence strip.

STRUCTURE
RallyCoach

Blacklines

Sentence Strips
Punctuation and Capitalization
RallyCoach

Instructions: Make a copy for each pair of students. Cut sentence strips apart.

1.	they are going to the zoo
2.	are you his mom
3.	can we go with you
4.	was that your cat
5.	i like my dog and cat
6.	all the pets were fed
7.	what will we do

Sentence Strips
Punctuation and Capitalization
RallyCoach
Instructions: Make a copy for each pair of students. Cut sentence strips apart.

8.	do you have one new book
9.	this is a fun day
10.	can I go with you
11.	he had to go home
12.	it is not from him
13.	we see your dad and mom
14.	were you going to the park

Sentence Strips
Punctuation and Capitalization Form
(Teacher-generated sentence strips)
RallyCoach

Instructions: Make a copy for each pair of students. Cut sentence strips apart.

1.

2.

3.

4.

5.

6.

7.

Sentence Strips
Punctuation and Capitalization Form
(Teacher-generated sentence strips)
RallyCoach

Instructions: Make a copy for each pair of students. Cut sentence strips apart.

8.

9.

10.

11.

12.

13.

14.

Checking My Writing
Sharing of Student Work

Checking My Writing

Six Trait Self-Assessment

The teacher's use of the Six Trait Question Strips in the modeled writing helps develop the student's awareness of the six trait skills and the value of checking one's work. The understanding will better enable students to self-monitor their own writing. After completing their writing, students will fill out the "Checking My Writing" form on the following page. After filling out the form, students should be encouraged and given opportunity to return to their work and revise as needed.

Sharing of Student Work

Mix-Pair-Share

One way to help students view themselves as writers is to have them share their writing with an authentic audience. Mix-Pair-Share is a structure that is designed to create a safe sharing environment between students.

Checking My Writing

Date: _____ Name: _____

Do I like my topic?	☺	☺	☹
Does my writing make sense when I read it?	☺	☺	☹
Did I use strong action words?	☺	☺	☹
Did I use describing words?	☺	☺	☹
Did I use a hook at the beginning?	☺	☺	☹
Is my paper easy to read?	☺	☺	☹
Does each sentence begin with a capital?	☺	☺	☹
Does each sentence end with punctuation?	☺	☺	☹

Checking My Writing

Date: _____ Name: _____

Do I like my topic?	☺	☺	☹
Does my writing make sense when I read it?	☺	☺	☹
Did I use strong action words?	☺	☺	☹
Did I use describing words?	☺	☺	☹
Did I use a hook at the beginning?	☺	☺	☹
Is my paper easy to read?	☺	☺	☹
Does each sentence begin with a capital?	☺	☺	☹
Does each sentence end with punctuation?	☺	☺	☹

Sharing Student Work

Students pair with classmates to share their writing.

Setup

• *Each student has a copy of his/her writing with the attached photograph.*

STRUCTURE
Mix-Pair-Share

Activity Steps

1. Students silently mix around the room.

2. Teacher calls, "Pair."

3. Students pair up with the person closest to them, who is not from their team, and do a high five. Students who haven't found a partner raise their hands to find each other.

4. Students take turns sharing their writing pieces by reading them to their partners using **RallyRobin**. Partners praise.

5. When both partners have shared their pieces, they thank each other and find a new partner and repeat from Step 3.

Index of Structures for Balanced Literacy

Structure

CenterPiece

Students brainstorm ideas, always trading their paper with the centerpiece.

Setup

• *Five pieces of paper per teams of four (one per person and one in the center)*

Steps

1. Teacher assigns a brainstorming topic.
2. Students generate items. They write one idea at a time and trade their paper with the one in the center.
3. Students continue brainstorming items, each time trading their paper with the centerpiece.

CenterPiece Activities and Blacklines

Find My Rule

Students induce a rule from examples provided by the teacher.

Steps

1. Teacher places one item in each area of the category frame.

2. Teacher asks, "What is my rule for placing items?" and provides think time.

3. Students RallyRobin with their shoulder partners to generate possible rules the teacher is using.

4. Teacher places two more objects in the category frame.

5. Teacher again says, "What is my rule?" and provides think time.

6. Students RallyRobin with their face partners to generate possible rules.

7. Teacher places more objects in the category frame, each time having teams discuss possible rules.

8. Teacher says, "Don't tell me your rule, name an item that fits in each category," and calls a number. Students with that number stand to share their items. The teacher confirms correct answers.

9. When most students seem to know the rule, the teacher calls on one student to verbalize the rule for the class.

10. Teacher confirms the rule.

11. Teacher presents new items one at a time, each time calling for students to hold up fingers indicating the category for the item.

12. Teacher congratulates the class.

Find My Rule Activities and Blacklines

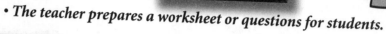

Structure

Find Someone Who

Students mix about the room, finding others who help them learn content or skills.

Setup

• *The teacher prepares a worksheet or questions for students.*

Steps

1. Students mix in the class, keeping a hand raised until they find a new partner that is not a teammate.

2. In pairs, Partner A asks a question from the worksheet; Partner B responds. Partner A records the answer on his or her own worksheet.

3. Partner B checks and initials the answer.

4. Partner B asks a question. Partner A responds. Partner B records the answer on his or her own worksheet.

5. Partner A checks and initials the answer.

6. Partners shake hands, part, and raise a hand again as they search for a new partner.

7. Students repeat Steps 1–6 until their worksheets are complete.

8. When their worksheets are completed, students sit down; seated students may be approached by others as a resource.

9. In teams, students compare answers; if there is disagreement or uncertainty, they raise four hands to ask a team question.

Find Someone Who Activities and Blacklines

Jot Thoughts

Teammates cover the table with ideas on slips of paper.

Steps

1. The teacher names a topic and sets a time limit.

2. Students announce and write as many ideas as they can in the allotted time, one idea per slip of paper.

3. Students attempt to cover the table with ideas (no slips are to overlap).

Jot Thoughts Activities and Blacklines

Listen-Sketch-Draft

Students sketch content chunk by chunk, create and compare main idea statements, and finally draft a summary statement.

Steps

1. Students listen while teacher presents the first chunk of information.

2. Teacher stops presenting and calls for each student to sketch the most important details.

3. Students share sketches using:
   • RoundRobin
   • Timed Pair Share

4. Students draft a main idea statement, based on the information shared in Step 1. While students draft their main ideas, teacher circulates and monitors.

5. The process is repeated for the next chunk.

6. When all chunks have been presented, students draft a summary statement.

7. Students compare their summaries with a partner or teammates praising ideas.

Listen-Sketch-Draft Activity and Blacklines

Structure

Mix-Pair-Share

Students pair with classmates to discuss questions posed by the teacher.

Setup

• *Teacher prepares discussion questions to ask students.*

Steps

1. Students silently mix around the room.

2. Teacher calls, "Pair."

3. Students pair up with the person closest to them and give a high five. Students who haven't found a partner raise their hands to find each other.

4. Teacher asks a question and gives think time.

5. Students share with their partners using:
   • Timed Pair Share
   • RallyRobin
   • RallyCoach

Mix-Pair-Share Activity

Numbered Heads Together

Teammates work together to ensure all members understand; one is randomly selected to be held accountable.

Setup

• *Teacher prepares questions or problems to ask teams.*

Steps

1. Students number off.

2. Teacher poses a problem and gives think time.
(Example: *Everyone think about how rainbows are formed.*)

3. Students privately write their answers.

4. Students lift up from their chairs to put their heads together, show answers, and discuss and teach.

5. Students sit down when everyone knows the answer or has something to share.

6. Teacher calls a number. The student with that number from each team answers simultaneously using:
   • Slate Share
   • Finger Responses
   • Response Cards
   • Choral Practice
   • Chalkboard Responses
   • Manipulatives

7. Teammates praise students who responded.

Numbered Heads Together Activities and Blacklines

Poems for Two Voices

Partners present a poem—recited at times by one partner, the other partner, or both.

Setup

- *The teacher prepares a poem with lines labeled A, B, or AB.*

Steps

1. Teacher explains and assigns students A and B roles.

2. Students read their labeled line, listening carefully to their partners to keep the flow.

Note: Students may progress through three stages:

1. Teacher provides poem and AB scripting.
2. Teacher provides poem and students provide AB scripting.
3. Students create or select poem and script it.

Poems for Two Voices Activities and Blacklines

Quiz-Quiz-Trade

Students quiz a partner, get quizzed by a partner, and then trade cards to repeat the process with a new partner.

Steps

1. StandUp–HandUp–PairUp
2. Partner A quizzes.
3. Partner B answers.
4. Partner A praises or coaches.
5. Switch roles.
6. Partners trade cards.
7. Repeat Steps 1–6 a number of times.

Quiz-Quiz-Trade Activities and Blacklines

Structure

RallyCoach

Partners take turns, one solving a problem while the other coaches.

Setup

- One set of high-consensus problems and one pencil per pair

Steps

1. Partner A solves the first problem.
2. Partner B watches and listens, checks, and praises.
3. Partner B solves the next problem.
4. Partner A watches and listens, checks, and praises.
5. Repeat starting at Step 1.

Note: RallyCoach may be used with worksheet problems, oral problems provided by the teacher, or manipulatives.

RallyCoach Activities and Blacklines

RallyCoach (continued)

Partners take turns, one solving a problem while the other coaches.

RallyCoach Activities and Blacklines

(continued on next page)

Structure

RallyCoach

Partners take turns, one solving a problem while the other coaches.

RallyCoach Activities and Blacklines

RallyRobin

In pairs, students alternate generating oral responses.

Steps

1. Teacher poses a problem to which there are multiple possible responses or solutions.

2. In pairs, students take turns stating responses or solutions.

RallyRobin Activities and Blacklines

RallyTable

In pairs, students alternate generating written responses or solving problems.

Setup

• *One paper and one pencil per pair*

Steps

1. Teacher poses a task to which there are multiple possible responses.

2. In pairs, students take turns passing the paper and pencil or pair project, each writing one answer or making a contribution.

   Variation: Simultaneous RallyTable. Students may each have their own piece of paper. Each writes at the same time and then trades at the same time.

RallyTable Activity and Blacklines

Structure

Showdown

Students answer questions without help. Teams then share, check, and coach.

Setup

- *Teams each have a set of question cards stacked facedown in the center of the table.*

Steps

1. Teacher selects one student on each team to be the Showdown Captain for the first round.
2. Showdown Captain draws the top card and reads the question.
3. Working alone, all students write their answers.
4. When finished, teammates signal when they are ready.
5. The Showdown Captain calls, "Showdown."
6. Teammates show and state their answers.
7. Showdown Captain leads the checking.
8. If correct, the team celebrates; if not, teammates coach, then celebrate.
9. The person on the left of the Showdown Captain becomes the Showdown Captain for the next round.

Showdown Activities and Blacklines

Simultaneous RallyTable

Students write, read, draw, solve problems, or practice something on their own.

Setup

• *Two papers and two pencils per pair*

Steps

1. Teacher assigns a topic or question and provides think time.
2. Both students respond, simultaneously writing, drawing, or building something with manipulatives.
3. The teacher signals time, or students place thumbs up when done with the problem.
4. Students pass papers or projects to partner clockwise.
5. Students continue, adding to what was already completed.
6. Continue, starting at Step 3.

Hint: Simultaneous RallyTable works well when each paper is labeled with a related topic (e.g., the four food groups, four historical characters).

Simultaneous RallyTable Activities and Blacklines

StandUp-HandUp-PairUp

Students stand up, put their hands up, and quickly find a partner with whom to share or discuss.

Steps

1. Teacher says, when I say go, you will "stand up, hand up, and pair up!" Teacher pauses, then says, "Go!"

2. Students stand up and keep one hand high in the air until they find the closest partner who's not a teammate. Students do a "high five" and put their hands down.

3. Teacher may ask a question or give an assignment, and provides think time.

4. Partners interact using:
   • RallyRobin
   • Timed Pair Share

Hint: In some classes, it may be necessary to make sure students pair with their classmate they are closest to rather than running to a friend.

StandUp-Hand-Up-PairUp Activity and Blacklines

Team Line-Ups

Students line up within their teams.

Setup

- *Teacher may prepare Line-Up cards or manipulatives for each team.*

Steps

1. Teacher gives teammates a problem.

2. Within their teams, teammates line up in order of their answers.

Team Line-Ups Activity and Blacklines

Timed Pair Share

In pairs, students share with a partner for a predetermined time while the partner listens. Then partners switch roles.

Steps

1. The teacher announces a topic, states how long each student will share, and provides think time.

2. In pairs, Partner A shares; Partner B listens.

3. Partner B responds with a positive gambit.

4. Partners switch roles.

Hint: The teacher provides positive response gambits to use in Step 3:

Copycat response gambits
- *"Thanks for sharing!"*
- *"You are interesting to listen to!"*

Complete the sentence gambits
- *"One thing I learned listening to you was…."*
- *"I enjoyed listening to you because…."*
- *"Your most interesting idea was…."*

Timed Pair Share Activity and Blacklines